THE CHANGING

Faringdon

and surrounding villages

**Rosemary Church,
Jim Brown, Millie Bryan
and Beryl Newman**

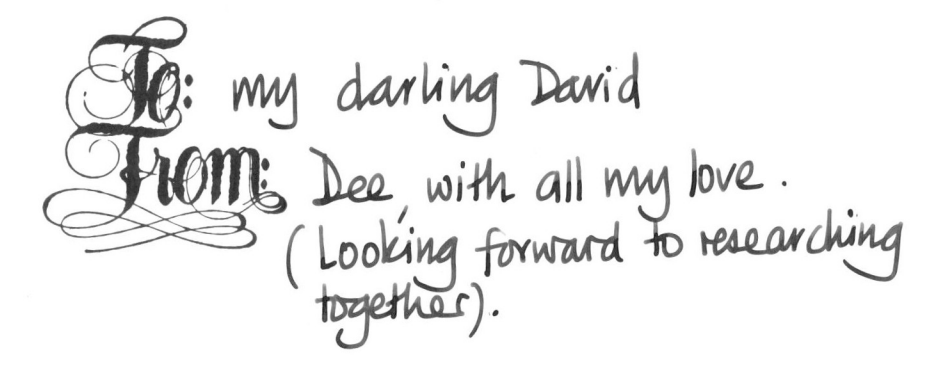

To: my darling David
From: Dee, with all my love.
(Looking forward to researching together).

Robert Boyd
PUBLICATIONS

Christmas
-1999-

Published by
Robert Boyd Publications
260 Colwell Drive
Witney, Oxfordshire OX8 7LW

First published 1999

Copyright © Rosemary Church,
Jim Brown, Millie Bryan, Beryl Newman,
Faringdon & District Historical Society and
Robert Boyd Publications

ISBN: 1 899536 45 0

All rights reserved. No part of this book may be produced, stored in a retrieval system, or transmitted, in any form or by any means, electronic, mechanical, photocopying, recording or otherwise, without the prior approval of the publisher.

TITLES IN THE *CHANGING FACES* SERIES

Banbury: Book One
The Bartons
Bicester: Book One *and* Book Two
Bladon with Church Hanborough and Long Hanborough
Botley and North Hinksey: Book One *and* Book Two
St Clements and East Oxford: Book One *and* Book Two
Cowley: Book One *and* Book Two
Cowley Works: Book One
Cumnor and Farmoor with Appleton and Eaton
St Ebbes and St Thomas: Book One *and* Book Two
Eynsham: Book One *and* Book Two
Faringdon and District
Grimsbury
Headington: Book One *and* Book Two
Iffley
Jericho: Book One *and* Book Two
Kennington
Littlemore and Sandford
Marston: Book One *and* Book Two
North Oxford: Book One *and* Book Two

Oxford City Centre: Book One
South Oxford: Book One *and* Book Two
Summertown and Cutteslowe
West Oxford
Witney: Book One
Wolvercote with Wytham and Godstow
Woodstock: Book One *and* Book Two
Yarnton with Cassington and Begbroke

FORTHCOMING

Abingdon
Banbury: Book Two
Blackbird Leys
Charlbury
Chipping Norton
Cowley: Book Three
Cowley Works: Book Two
Easington
Florence Park
Grimsbury: Book Two
Littlemore and Sandford: Book Two
Oxford City Centre: Book Two
Rose Hill
Thame
Witney: Book Two

Printed and bound in Great Britain at The Alden Press, Oxford

Contents

Introduction		4
Map of the area		6
Section 1	Faringdon Streets	7
Section 2	Business	27
Section 3	Faringdon Church, House and Folly	44
Section 4	Events	49
Section 5	The Market	57
Section 6	Personalities	60
Section 7	Public Houses	66
Section 8	Schools	72
Section 9	Societies and Sports	82
Section 10	Transport	91
Section 11	Views	95
Section 12	Buscot	97
Section 13	Coleshill	100
Section 14	Great Coxwell	102
Section 15	Little Coxwell	105
Section 16	Eaton Hastings	107
Section 17	Fernham	108
Section 18	Shellingford	113
Section 19	Uffington	121

Cover illustrations

Front: From the top of Faringdon Church, looking south over Market Place.

Back: Shellingford, c.1905. The boy on the horse is Arthur Pill. He was killed in action in France on Aug 18th 1916, aged 19 years.
The White Horse public house at Woolstone, in the early 1900s. The photograph is taken from the little farmyard opposite.

Acknowledgements

We had a large number of photographs to choose from and our choice probably differs from that of other people. We would like to offer our apologies if you think that we should have included a particular photograph, but we had limited space in the book. The authors would like to thank the following people for their help and advice with photographs and captions.

Brian Brady; Betty O'Brien for the illustrated map; John Carter; Eileen Eyles; Faringdon & District Historical Society; Pat Fox, Girl Guides; Chris France; Colin Franklin, Boy Scouts; Peter Hunt; Ken Hutt; Di Mander; Pat Perkins, Tennis Club; Nancy Reeves; Tim Reeves, Dramatic Society; *Swindon Evening Advertiser*; Mary Venn; Joan Wood. Jean Cole for checking and amending the text.

We are also grateful for permission to use extracts from *A History of the Old Berks Hunt 1760–1904* by F. C. Loder-Symonds and E. Percy Crowdy, which was published in 1905.

Introduction

Recent discoveries in the Faringdon area have found evidence of occupation by Iron Age people and the Romans. The evidence for Saxon occupation is very sparse as Saxon pottery does not last well in the soil in this area, but excavations at Lechlade and Shrivenham have revealed large, wealthy Anglo-Saxon communities. The Vale of the White Horse lay on the border of the Kingdom of Wessex and just south of the Kingdom of Mercia so the area must have been involved in disputes over territory. At the time of the Norman Conquest King Harold owned the manor of Faringdon and then it came into the hands of the Norman kings. In 1203 King John gave the Cistercian Order the manor, including a piece of land at Wyke, on which to build a monastery. The monks erected some buildings, the remains of which were re-discovered a few years ago. However the monks didn't stay for long as they preferred a site that was more remote from centres of population. The Cistercians moved to Beaulieu, leaving Faringdon and Great Coxwell to become granges for the collection of agricultural produce. The produce was sold and the proceeds sent to Beaulieu. The Great Barn at Great Coxwell dates from this time and it is likely that a similar building was extant at Faringdon. Beaulieu Abbey continued to hold land in Faringdon until the dissolution of the monasteries in the 16th century. Other large, local landowners have been some of the Oxford colleges. Oriel College owned Wadley, Littleworth, Wicklesham and parts of Faringdon. Brasenose College owned parts of Port and Westbrook in Faringdon.

Faringdon's importance came from the crossing of two ancient ways: one from London, via Oxford and Abingdon, to Cirencester and on to Gloucester and South Wales, or to Bristol, Bath and Somerset; the other from the North of England, via Coventry and Burford, to Marlborough, Winchester and Southampton. In the Civil War Faringdon became a garrison town protecting King Charles and his forces at Oxford. There were several small skirmishes in the area and in 1644 Oliver Cromwell led an attack on Faringdon House, where the garrison was ensconced, but failed to subdue it.

The garrison finally surrendered to the Parliamentarian forces on June 24th 1646, being one of the last places to do so. During the war the church and the town had been extensively damaged and in 1648 the townsfolk asked Parliament for compensation, the damage being assessed at £56,976 4s, but this was refused.

Faringdon's position at the western end of the Vale of the White Horse led to it becoming a thriving market for the sale of agricultural and animal produce. It was especially known for the sale of cheese and pigs. In the journal of Thomas Baskerville he mentions passing through Faringdon and that 'a great fair for horses, cattle and other goods, was held here on Whitsun Tuesday and that there were many inns in the town, the chief of which was the Crown.' In 1813 'there was a great quantity of swine fatted in Berkshire and Faringdon slaughters 4,000 pigs for the London and Oxford markets between the beginning of November and the beginning of April.' About 8,000 sides were smoked annually in Faringdon before being sent to market. Edward Loveden's dairy farm, at Buscot, used its surplus milk to rear the Berkshire black pigs and he sold them as breeding stock throughout the world. The Market Hall, built in the late 17th or early 18th century, was used to sell butter, eggs and farm produce on market days.

Faringdon was connected by Turnpike roads to London and Gloucester by 1733 and to Wantage and Wallingford in 1752. By 1813 coaches were passing through Faringdon from the West Country on their way to London every Tuesday, Thursday and Saturday. The Wilts and Berks canal was first proposed in 1793 but it took until 1810 for it to brought right across the Vale. It was 52 miles long and was mainly used to carry coal from Somerset, but it also carried stone, salt and agricultural products. The canal was navigable to the wharf at Longcot by December 1805. Other wharves were built at Challow, Uffington and Wantage. The canal suffered severely when the Great Western Railway Company built stations close to the wharves and took away its trade. The Faringdon Branch Railway, under private ownership, was opened in June 1864. By 1869 between 150 and 180 churns of milk a week left the station to join the main line at Uffington. However the branch was not a success and in 1886 the Faringdon Railway Company ceased to exist and the line was transferred to the G.W.R. It was eventually closed to passengers in 1951 and finally to freight traffic on July 1st 1963.

It is unknown when All Saints Church was founded, it was certainly here at the recording of the Domesday Book in 1086. Parts of the present building date from the 12th century, with work being carried out in the following centuries. The church came under the jurisdiction of the Diocese of Salisbury. The Anabaptists were founded in Faringdon in 1576. Baptists had an official church here in 1657 but may well have had a company of believers here in the previous century. The Congregational Church, in Marlborough St., was built in 1840 to replace a small chapel erected in 1799. The Wesleyan Chapel, in Gloucester St., was built in 1837. The Primitive Methodists Chapel, in Coxwell St., was built in 1896. The Quakers were established in the area in the middle of the 17th century and a Meeting House, one of the earliest in the region, was built in Faringdon by the 1670s; the present building is thought to date from 1696.

Rosemary Church
April 1999

Map of the area. (Drawn by Betty O'Brien.)

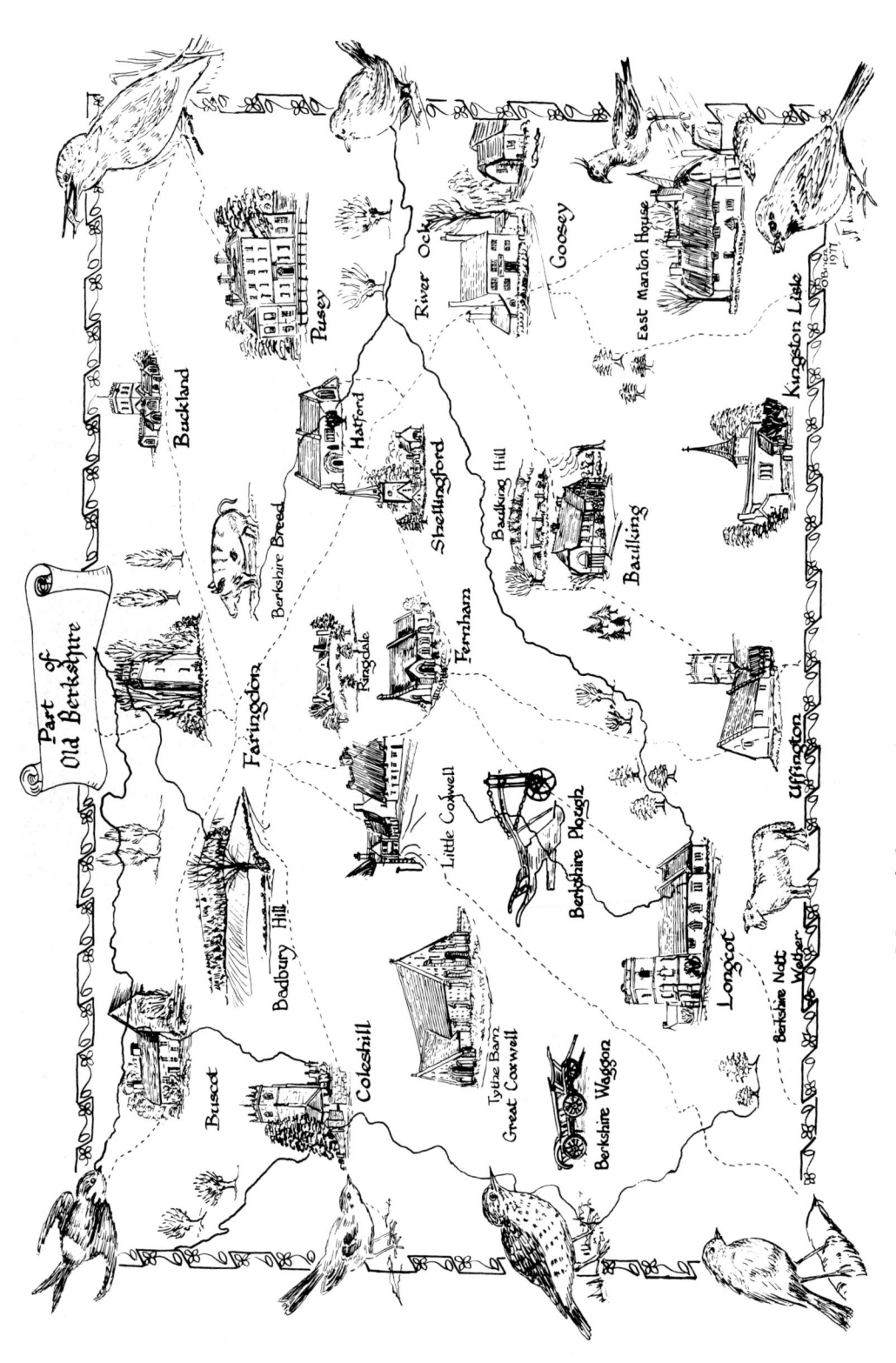

SECTION ONE

Faringdon Streets

Bromsgrove

1911, June 22nd Coronation of King George V. Looking from Christopher Square towards Bromsgrove. The street is en fête for the Coronation celebrations and everyone is dressed in their best. The Swan Inn is off the picture on the right and the Baptist Chapel is off the picture on the left hand corner. The children are able to pose in the middle of the street as there was no danger from traffic. The child on the left is Dick 'Jammy' James. The third person from the right is Mr Harry Whipp; fifth from the right is Mr Harris, head tailor for Pocock, and left of him is his son.

1953, looking towards the Swan Inn. The Baptist Chapel is on the right and the cottages seen in the last picture are on the left. The street is still very quiet and lacking in vehicles. A car can be seen passing along Station Rd (now Park Rd) in front of Eagle Motors car repair workshop and stores. This used to be Clare's Coaches. Tommy Clare started up with an ex-Army lorry at the end of WWI doing haulage and later on branched out into coach travel. The buildings have been demolished and the area is now a small estate called the Eagles. The house on the right, with the two upper windows visible, has also been demolished and the site has been made into a small public garden.

1880s, at the junction with Marlborough St. The house on the left, with the chequerboard brickwork, was built by Hughes Bros., painters, paperhangers and bell hangers. The building next to it is Top Goddard's which was a haberdashery shop and at this time the owner was probably William Collins Sell who was listed as a linen and woollen draper, silk mercer, hatter, hosier and agent for sewing machines. The drawers and storage units that he would have used are still preserved in the present day restaurant.

Church Street

Early 1900s, looking along Church St. from the Market Place. The Salutation Inn is on the right with the viacarage next to it. The churchyard wall is on the left.

1953, looking from the Radcot Rd. Church Farm House is where the bushes are growing over the wall, the farm buildings being on both sides of the road. The archway on the left leads into the yard belonging to Mr Lister, a builder. The previous owners were Cadel's the builders who were responsible for erecting much of the Marlborough Gardens Estate.

1953. These buildings belonged to Faringdon House and were used for servant accommodation. The archway was a carriage entrance to the original Faringdon House.

1953. The view of Church St from the Radcot Road. Bleak House, which had been a cheese warehouse, is on the left next to the entrance of Coach Lane. Next door was originally the coach house and stable for the adjacent house called The Grove. This building was occupied by Mr Crowdy, solicitor, and later became Dr Pulling's surgery. One of the rooms in The Grove had two large cupboards with iron doors (installed during the time of the solicitor's practice for holding important and private documents). These cupboards were used by Dr Pulling for his drugs and medicines.

Corn Market

An 1890s view of a corner of the Corn Market and looking up Marlborough St. The first shop on the left is Mr Edwin Counsell's shop and home, then known as Waltham House in honour of his being an agent for the American Waltham watches. He sold jewellery and spectacles as well as maintaining his watch and clock repair business. The large clock, with the works hidden in a cupboard by the side of the window, was made by one of his ancestors. The man standing at the entrance to Brewery Alley is George Pill, a brewery worker, wearing the sacking apron to protect his clothes. Next door is the Red Lion public house. Mr Henry Godfrey was the landlord and also the proprietor of the Faringdon Brick & Tile works on the Stanford Road. Adjoining the Red Lion is Faringdon's new Post Office, which for some years had been run from a house opposite the Portwell Pump in the Market Place. On the opposite side of the road is Mr Westall's bakery delivery cart with the roundsman standing by. Lane Bros.'s sign over their premises dominates the skyline. They dealt in almost everything. At one time they had an advertising slogan 'anything from a pin to an elephant supplied.' Beneath these signs the protruding shop window belonged to Goulding Goddard's, another outfitter's shop. On the right is the International Tea Co. shop with a farmer's trap parked outside.

1920s. The International Tea Co. shop has the sun blind down to protect the goods in their window display. The Corn Exchange has finished as a farmers' dealing centre and is now Faringdon's first cinema with the best seats in the house costing 3d (just over 1p). The auctioneer's gallery was commonly called 'the cuddly corner' as it was frequented by the young couples, these seats cost 6d (2½p). The gallery also held the store of rat-infested grain sacks, much to the detriment of any budding romance. Saturday morning sessions were also held at the cinema when youngsters could get in, to see such films as the Pearl White thrillers, for the price of 2d.

1953. The International Tea Co. shop has given way to E. Leverton & Sons, outfitters and furniture shop. The Leverton family also owned Mr Counsell's shop on the other side of the Corn Market, which was run by Mr David Leverton. Note the advertising sign for Bush radios and the one between the windows advertising Wellington Boots. The Corn Exchange is now being fully used as a public hall for dances, dinners and meetings. Bridge Turf Accountants was run by Mr F. Bowerman from an office at the front. The plaque commemorates Queen Elizabeth II's Coronation in 1952.

Early 1930s. On the left is White Bros. Mr George White was first recorded in London St in 1844 and then in 1854 in Gloucester St and he was listed as a haircutter and perfumer. At this time it is two brothers doing the hairdressing but there is also a ladies hairdressing salon on the first floor. Next is Wyle Bros. boot and shoe shop; they were one of the oldest continuous businesses in Faringdon for some time. This shop was first recorded as the Leeds & Leicester Shoe Company and later they changed their name to Wyle's and finally closed in the 1970s. Next is a little private house, then comes Mr Yeatman, who used to advertise as a breeches maker, outfitter and tailor. He was first recorded in 1895. One of the traps in front of the buildings is Mr Viner's from Smokedown Farm who is in town shopping with his wife.

Coxwell Road/Coxwell Street

Early 1900s. Faringdon Cottage Hospital on the left. Note the unmade road with the horse and trap approaching.

1905. The Cottage Hospital was erected in 1892. Captain Dundas initiated public subscriptions to help build it and contributed a considerable amount of the money required. The first Matron was Miss Rosa Broughton. The medical officers were J.P. Lockwood, H.D. Ley and C. Spackman; the consulting surgeon was H.P. Symonds from Oxford. The hospital was comprised of two wards of two beds each, one for women and one for men; two private wards of one bed each, one male and one female; matron's sitting room and an office. Later on there was an operating room and a morgue. The first major operation was for Mrs Elliott, wife of the Saw Mills proprietor, who had a burst appendix. A well-loved matron, in later years, was Gertrude Taylor, sister to Percy Taylor the butcher.

1990. Quarry Engineering on the left through the iron gates. Previous owners were Ballard & Sons, blacksmith and wheelwright, who occupied it from at least 1895. They were followed by Frank Lane, D.W. Lansdown and Quarry Engineering before being used for housing (now called Nichol Court). Nearby was the site of Faringdon's last Toll Gate which was demolished when a haulier was driving home from Swindon late at night. The man was very drunk and fell asleep on the cart and so the horse failed to stop and walked straight through the Toll Gate.

1912. The crossroads at the end of Coxwell St. On the left is the Methodist Church next to the Duke of York, licencee Michael Giannadrea. The inn was demolished and the new United Church now stands there. The left-hand turning is Gravel Walk, on the far side of it can be seen the White Hart with its inn sign standing on the corner. The road facing is Marlborough St. showing how the road is cut away at Arthurs Hill. To the right is Station Rd (now Park Rd) leading to the railway station.

Gloucester Street

Looking towards the town centre. On the left is Thomas Hicks the bakers and general store. Next is Price's motor cycle showroom (later part of Enterprise Garage group) run by Maurice Musselwhite. The next house was the home of Mr Liles the piano tuner. This later became a hairdresser's run by Eileen Gibbs, and is now a private house. Then the Elms School, with the headmistress' house in the front. This has become part of Faringdon Junior School and Faringdon County Library. The last house to be seen is Elmside, which was demolished and rebuilt as flats.

1953. Langford's Corn Stores, on the left, was originally a barn belonging to a farm with the dairy on the opposite side of the road. Seeds, gardening items, pet foods, etc. were sold there. It has recently been converted into flats. Gloucester House, the dentist's surgery, is fronted by trees and bushes. It is thought that this was the old farm house of the farm that stood there many years ago. Further along is the cinema where once stood some barns and old cottages belonging to the farm. White Bros. hairdressing establishment, where the sunblind is protruding, was also a tobacconist. At the end of the street can be seen the fishmonger's shop.

Gravel Walk

1953. View from the Junction with Lechlade Rd. The house on the right, known as Chase House, has the wall round its garden. The end near to the road to the Town Pound (now the entrance to the Bowls Club) was once a stable with a store above it. Note the water stand pipe on the right. At this time some people were still using it to obtain their water.

FARINGDON STREETS 17

1982. The same view as the previous photograph. The shop window on the right is Motor Parts owned by Ian Stringer. The garden wall has since disappeared and the garden has been made into a parking area for Motor Parts. The house was previously occupied by Mr. and Mrs. Indge, coal merchant and hairdresser. Many old Faringdon families have lived in Gravel Walk, e.g. Druett; Flo and Sid King; Gerring; Rixon; Harris; Mr. and Mrs. P. Cox; Pocock; Abel (jewellers); Jim Brown (carrier).

1910. The White Hart is on the right. Just in front of it can be seen a small building which was the public weigh-bridge. The buildings behind have had a variety of uses including storage, Boffin's butcher's shop and an antique centre. All these old premises, including the weigh-bridge, have now been demolished to make way for a block of flats.

Lechlade Road

1982. The large showroom window on the left was originally the site of A.E. Baker & Sons, blacksmith, wheelwright and monumental masons. The last blacksmith was Cecil Drew and the last mason was Ken Baker. It became a car showroom, then a pine furniture shop and finally an antique centre, Auntie's Emporium. The next house is the Ilott family home, previously a small sweet shop run by Mrs. Hunt and followed by her daughter Mrs Ilott. The Wellington public house comes next, then the Enterprise Garage which, by 1988, was replaced by private flats. The other side of Canada Lane is the present day Infant School.

1982. The junction of Lechlade Rd, Gloucester St and Gravel Walk.

London Street

1910. A Henry Taunt view of London St. Possibly a market day because of the number of people around. The building on the left is the office of Haines the solicitors, now the Cheltenham & Gloucester Building Society. The shop window halfway up on the right is Chamberlain's grocery shop, beyond is a bow window belonging to Hughes' the paper shop. The Bell Hotel is on the right-hand edge of the picture. Beyond is a draper's shop, owned by Creese & Co. in 1895, later occupied by Luker, printer, then the Ann family, ironmonger, and then Sam Burge, saddler.

1930. The cycle shop on the left frequently changed owners, amongst which were Yates & Sons, Rigden, Geary and Huxley. Further up the street is the 'Wheatsheaf' public house; Jamieson, tailor (later the Electricity Board Showroom); Moyne, ironmonger; Comley, furniture; the junction with Swan Lane; 'Marlborough' public house; Obourn, shoe shop and hairdressers. The ironmonger's on the right is in the occupation of Mr Percy Thomas; this was later taken over by Mr Moyne. During WWII it was a sweet shop called Shenton's.

Market Place

c.1880s. The east side of Market Place with London Street on the right. The entrance to Haines' premises, who was a solicitor and also ran a postal lending library, was the doorway that can be seen just in London Street. From the right is Cooper, Chymist; Lay, baker and confectioner; the County of Gloucester Bank; Liddiard, grocer; George Ernest, grocer and bacon curer. Most of these buildings had a separate passageway, from the Market Place, to gain access to the living accommodation, plus one from Swan Lane to the buildings used for the storage of goods and the stabling of horses.

1880s. Looking at the same side of the Market Place from near the church. From the left is Pettifer, the builder's; these premises were eventually taken over by the Salutation Hotel. Next comes a barber's, shown by the barber's pole outside the shop. Under the overhang was a sweet shop where the lady owner would serve customers through the window but wouldn't allow them inside. The four white squares above the ground floor windows of Pump House are where the letters BANK were chiselled out when the County of Gloucester Bank moved there. The building was then used as offices by the Eagle Brewery followed by a club for ex-servicemen before becoming the Community Centre. The building where there is a protruding window was Liddiard's grocery stores. The Portwell can be seen on the right-hand side.

The Portwell was given to the town in the 16th century by Sir Henry Unton. It was used for providing water for the horses and cattle that used the market. The troughs were on the west and south sides, while on the north side there was a pump with a drinking bowl for people to use. The gas lamps were placed on top in the 19th century.

1910s. The Town Hall has had a chequered history and at one time was used as a lock-up for prisoners awaiting trial. The fire engine was kept underneath. Note the wooden framework on the side which was used for drying the hoses and the bell on the roof used for summoning the firemen. The Church bier was stored there and, during WWII, it was commandeered by the army for accommodating soldiers. In recent times it has variously been a meeting room, a library and finally a Red Cross Charity shop. Ann's Garage is visible to the left of the Town Hall. This was taken over by Busby, newsagents, and now belongs to Dillon's. On the left, at the junction with Southampton Street, is Pocock, tailor, which has now become part of Barclay's Bank. The bell hanging outside the Bell Hotel can just be seen on the left of the picture. The gas lamps are hanging outside the draper's shop.

1953. The Church can be seen at the top of the picture. On the right is the Salutation Hotel with Crowdy and Rose, solicitors, next door. Then comes the butcher's shop, owned at various times by Heavens, Boycott and Wright. Next is the hardware and china shop owned by A. E. Lismore who also ran a converted bus to sell goods and paraffin to the outlying villages. The last building on the right is the Community Centre. This had been the County of Gloucester Bank but was given to the town by Lord Faringdon for a peppercorn rent to be used as an ex-serviceman's club. Opposite is the corner of Portwell House which was formerly the Angel Inn and Post Office.

Marlborough Street

1916. Looking from the Corn Market. The Corn Exchange can be seen on the right and was originally used for the sale local produce. Later it was used as a cinema and nowadays for a variety of functions. In 1997 a licence was granted to enable marriages to be performed there. The International Stores faces the Corn Market. On the left is the Red Lion with the Post Office next, followed by Carter's grocery store.

FARINGDON STREETS 23

1928. In the doorway of Carter's is Mr Cyril Carter. The arched windows behind him was a café. The shop on the right, which juts out, was Goulding Goddard's drapers, which later became Larkin's electrical shop, and presently Reflections, a craft shop.

c. 1914. An early picture looking down Marlborough Street towards the Corn Market or the Narrows. At the bottom of the street, on the right, is the Post Office with Carter's grocery store next to it. Near the front of the picture is the wall bordering the Congregational Chapel, which is now the Roman Catholic Church. The person bending over the bicycle could be mending a puncture, a regular hazard at this time due to the condition of the roads. Counsell's clock is visible outside what is now the Nut Tree.

Late 1950s. The top end of Marlborough Street showing Arthurs Hill. Note the lack of traffic and people. Today there is a continuous line of cars parked on the left-hand side. At the corner of Bromsgrove and Marlborough Street, on the left-hand side of the picture, is the grocery shop belonging to Mr Manners. On the right are shop fronts of a butcher's and the Co-op, all now demolished. The Police Station and Telephone Exchange now stand on this site.

An early picture of Arthur's Hill. The road had to be deepened during the coaching era to ease the horses' load up the steep gradient. The hill was named after H. N. Arthur, a coach and harness maker, whose business is shown on the right of the picture. The building was taken over by Frank Lane's carpenter shop and during WWII was used to house the ambulance; today it is an antique centre. Next door was the home of Mr Smith who was the first recorded professional photographer in Faringdon. The adjacent cottage became Ron Young's barber's shop before he moved into London Street. The large house at the end of the rank is Marlborough House. The house facing, at the junction of Bromsgrove, later became a shop and had a variety of owners such as Billy Long, Chapman, Paddon and Manners. Recently it has been a pet shop and finally today it is a shop selling second-hand items. To the right of the house can be seen the edge of the draper's shop owned by the Goddard family and known as 'Top Goddards'. The shop changed hands and was owned in turn by Colin Sell, then Mr Fish and Mr Geoff until, finally, it was converted into a restaurant called the Rat's Castle.

Southampton Street

1953. Worlds End, Southampton Street. The building on the left was occupied by the Long and Arlott families, the latter being cook and caretaker for the school. The White Horse Dairy is next on the left. The long wall on the right is the boundary wall of Liddiards Row cottages and gardens.

1953. The rows of cottages were occupied by many old Faringdon families, for example Archer; Barnes; Timms; Long; Phillips; Haynes; Greenaway. All of this was demolished to make way for the Pitts Estate and the Lees — Westbrook and Portway Estate.

The last house on the left was the home of Mr. & Mrs. Frank Long; Jane Long had a small sweet shop there. It was later taken over by Mrs Phillips. Mr Phillips came to Faringdon in a strange way. Mr Porter, of the Corn Stores in Gloucester Street, was one of the first people in Faringdon to buy a car and, as he was frightened to drive it, he decided to go by train to London and ask the first taxi driver he met to become his chauffeur. This he did and Mr Phillips came to live in Faringdon. However, after marrying and becoming the father of three children, he died, so Mr Porter set up his widow in the sweet shop in order that she might earn a living. The last occupants were Mrs. Bayly and family. Next was Cadel's stable and cart house (note the feed loft). The building with the long, low roof was the monumental masons, carpenters and painters shed and was owned firstly by Cadel, then Mr. Reason and finally Russell Spinage.

1967. Redevelopment of Southampton Street. Driving piles for the foundations of Ferngrove sheltered accommodation. Immediately behind the pile driver is Russell Spinage's yard. This area was originally the gardens between Southampton Street and Bromsgrove. It was very low-lying with a stream in the bottom. The stream was used by a leather tannery run by Bailey Bros., but has been piped and runs under the Narrows of the Corn Market and into the lake of Faringdon House.

SECTION TWO

Business

1916. Carters in Marlborough Street (now Budgens). The shop was owned by four generations of the Carter family – John, Albert, Cecil, John and Norman, until it was sold in 1996. The shop was a grocery, butchers, paraffin and corn stores. Deliveries were made to all the surrounding villages, firstly with horse and cart and later with motor vans. In Carter's at this time the counters went round the sides of the shop and assistants served the customer over this counter. The bill was paid at a small wooden kiosk just inside the door. The men all wore long white aprons and this continued until well into the 1950s. The Carter family lived over the shop; note the lace curtains in one of the upstairs windows. When John and Norman took over the shop they gradually enlarged the business, taking over the shop next door which had housed Jack o'Newbury's cleaners. On the retirement of Mr Percy Taylor from his butcher's shop in the Corn Market the premises were purchased by Carter's who continued to run it as a butchers and slaughter house. The meat business moved back into the main shop and the premises extended at the back. The small building on the right of the picture was the office for the shop. Previously this had been a café run by Cyril Carter's sisters, Phyllis Johnson and Kathleen Hogan. They eventually moved to the bakery in the Market Place (Lays) which became Hogan's. Albert Carter is the man outside in the bowler hat. Young Cyril Carter was driving the delivery trap as, during the war, labour was scarce so he had to help out whenever he could.

A photograph of some 40 members out of the total of over 90 staff of Carter's taken in September 1996. This photograph was presented to John and Norman Carter upon the occasion of the sale of their shop. They were presented with a copy, together with individual photo albums of all the staff, at a farewell party at Sudbury House. Left to right: Barry Townsend; Bridget Dean; Milly Bryan; Grace Hook; Ruth Cox; Ann Griffiths; Barbara Timpson; Doreen Leslie; Jim Cave; Linda Leggett; Judy Wickham; Barbara Wood; Fred Robins; Maureen Ellis; Jenny Townsend; Mervyn Carter; Sandra Bishop; Shirley Jennings; Jean Wooster; Barbara Cornish; Wendy Sly; Pat Church; Brian Hudson; Mark Winteringham; Karen Pill; Jo Ride; Linda Hughes; Denise Law; Erin Wood; Sarah Priest; Alex Bagshall; Jenny Rimmer; Mary Joyce; Janet Rees; Duncan Saunders; Tina Cronin; Micky Uzzel; Mandy Spencer; Stacey Wright; Brian Carter.

1953 The Post Office in Marlborough Street. It was built in 1898 when the building housing Taylor's fish shop was demolished. The small building at the end was used as a storeroom by Carter's until it was demolished when the shop became a supermarket. The enamel signs on the facing wall of Bicester House (Carter's) have been removed, thanks to pressure from Mrs Cyril Carter.

c.1880s. Mr Taylor's butcher's shop was the shop between the Volunteer Inn in Gloucester Street and the opticians in Corn Market. In the picture the carcasses of the prize winners in the Christmas Fat Stock Show are displayed. Mr Taylor with the hat and Mr Wareham, the butcher, on the right.

OUR MEAT DEPARTMENT.

OUR FISH, GAME AND POULTRY DEPARTMENT.

TAYLOR & SONS, Purveyors, Faringdon, BERKS.

1910. The top picture is the front of the same premises as the last picture. This shop was sold to Carter's in 1959. The bottom picture is of the fishmonger's shop in the Narrows between the Corn Market and Market Place. The sign over the shop was transferred from their previous premises in Marlborough Street. The shop front has been glazed, but apart from this, the premises, including the marble slab used for displaying the fish, remained the same until 1999. The shop was owned by the Taylor family until 1959 when it was sold to Mr Rogers. He later sold it on and it finally closed as a fishmonger's in 1998. The brook that separated Westbrook from Port runs under this shop in a culvert and then goes under the road.

1911. The International Stores which was next to the Corn Exchange. The shop was moved to the Narrows, between the Corn Market and the Market Place, next to the present newspaper shop. Staff, left to right: Dolman (cashier); Blake? (manager); Samways; Talbot; Jesse Weaver.

c.1920. Mr Harry Abel outside his watchmaker and jewellery shop. This is still a jewellers' shop and the frontage has remained largely unchanged. Abel Bros had owned a shop in the Market Place from at least 1877.

1912. The Anns family had been, since at least 1824, ironmongers, gun retailers and repairers in London Street. At the arrival of the car they set up a garage in Market Place (where Hobbs and Chambers are now). Following this they bought Mr Newman's blacksmiths shop across the road. Left to right: Harry Robins, head mechanic; Edgar Argent, apprentice.

c.1908. On the left is Joseph Newman, blacksmith, who had been here from at least 1877. His forge was at the rear of the house and horses had to be taken through the passageway on the right. These premises were converted into a garage by the Anns family. On the right is Taylor's, a greengrocer's, and a member of the fishmonger and butcher family. The large board, by the window, is covered in photographs taken by Mr E. Haworth of Gloucester Street, Faringdon's leading photographer.

BUSINESS 33

Early 1930s. Market Place. Robey's sold vegetables and dairy produce. The shop was taken over by Jane's Pantry during WWII and stayed until the 1960s. It is now a restaurant.

1950s. In front of the cinema in Gloucester St. Jean Purbrick with Eric Morbey who worked at the Regent Petrol Depot in the railway station yard as a driver's mate. He had been a delivery boy at Carter's when he was a schoolboy.

1984. The Regent Cinema, previously the Rialto Cinema, which was built in 1935/6 to replace barns and old farm cottages. It was opened by Lord Berners who made the longest speech of his career, all twelve words of it. The first film shown was 'Life of the Bengal Lancers'. There was such a crush that an usherette fainted and had to be carried out over the heads of the crowd. The cinema, later a Bingo Hall, has now been replaced by the housing development known as Regent Mews.

1986, Market Place. Mortons in the year of its closure. This was a shop selling an assortment of goods — bicycles, clothes, haberdashery and toys. It was well known that you could go into Swindon to buy something, fail to get it and come back to Mortons and find it. Previously this belonged to Wilkes. The shop has now been split into two, the video shop on the right and an Indian take-away on the left.

1931, Chamberlain's grocery store (now the off licence) in London Street. Left to right: Arthur Shurmer; Leslie Pauling; Dorothy Bowerman; Betty Willis; Jim Egleton; Ted Newdick; Jack Bryan (his first day at work). This was a very high-class grocer, the smell of freshly ground coffee would linger in the street tempting customers inside. The shop was rebuilt c.1938 and the frontage moved back to its present position. The Co-op moved here for a short time when their premises in Marlborough Street were demolished to make way for the Police Station and Telephone Exchange.

BUSINESS   35

1939–45, Chamberlain's staff. Left to right: Joan Goodhart; Jean MacDonald; Nora Carter; Dorrie Imms; Gladys Skinner; Audrey Hartley; Rose Palmer; in the front an American G.I. The shop was mainly staffed by ladies as most of the men had gone off to the war.

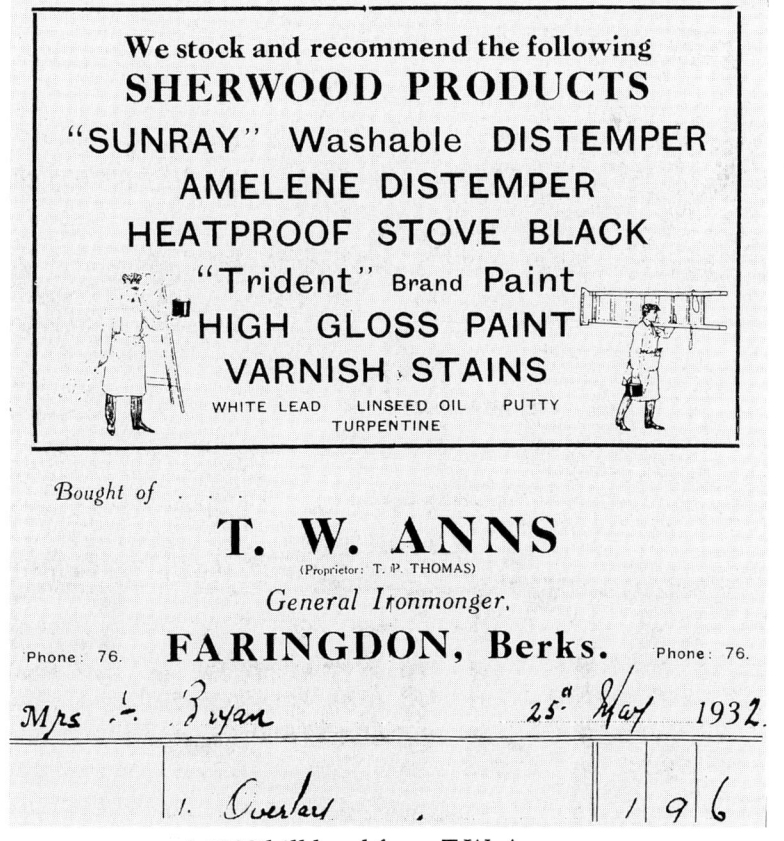

A 1932 bill head from T.W. Anns.

Nº 6243

Bought of . . .

E. LEVERTON & SONS
CORNMARKET, FARINGDON, BERKS.

Boots and shoes	Ladies' and Gents' Underclothing	Carpets and Rugs
Dressmaking and Millinery	Gloves and Umbrellas	Jewellery, Watches and Clocks
Coats and Costumes	Ready Made Clothing	Watch and Clock Repairs
Suits made to Measure and Ready Made	Waterproofs and Showerproofs	Gem Rings
Silks and Furs	Shirts and Collars	Wireless Sets
Dress Materials and Prints	Matting, Bedding and Linoleums, Furniture	Wireless Parts
Ladies' and Children's Dresses		Batteries Charged
		Wireless Sets Repaired
		Electrical Goods
		Electric Wiring and Repairs

Phone: Faringdon 2161

CUSTOMERS' VEHICLES ARE DRIVEN OR STORED BY US ENTIRELY AT OWNER'S RISK

THE ENTERPRISE GARAGES
R. A. PRICE, M.I.M.T. PROPRIETOR.

Faringdon, Berks.

TELEPHONE 69

LIGHT CAR AND MOTOR CYCLE SPECIALISTS. NEW AND USED.

Mrs Bryan   2nd April 1938

To One Second hand Ford 8 H.P. Saloon Car J.B.2461
as seen tried and approved; including tyres & repairs.   47 10 0
Third Party Insurance.   4   0 0
Licence to 30/6/38.   1 13 0
                                                     £   53   3 0

BOUGHT OF

GOULDING & CO.
Proprietor: JOSEPH GODDARD

DRAPERS, MILLINERS
AND OUTFITTERS

Marlborough Street, Faringdon

A collection of bill heads from various shops in Faringdon at different periods of time.

BUSINESS 37

1986, looking from All Saints churchyard across Church Street towards Swan Lane. Enterprise Garage is on the left of Swan Lane and separated from it by the garden of the vicarage (where the trees and bushes are). Mrs Parker used to keep geese there. The sites of the garage and garden were sold for redevelopment and are now sheltered housing. The old vicarage is on the right of Swan Lane.

The staff of Cadel Bros., builders in Church Street. Seated second from left is Johnny Croome. Jack Sellwood is in the foreground.

1951, D.J. Elliott & Sons Sawmills in Station Road. This is the occasion of the annual boiler overhaul, de-scale and flue clean, during the Sawmills annual holiday. It was a ship's boiler and came from Liverpool to the Buscot Dairy next door to the Sawmills. The Dairy was purchased by the Express Dairy who enlarged and modernised it. Mr Elliott bought the boiler from them and the intervening walls were demolished to enable the boiler to be rolled into its new position. To supply the steam for the mill, the boiler consumed waste wood and sawdust plus a truck-load of coal per week. In the later 1950s, the boiler failed an inspection test. It was cut up for scrap and the steam engine was dismantled and sold to a lace factory in Nottingham. The mill was Faringdon's biggest employer. It finally closed in 1961 when the Express Dairy purchased the premises. The men standing in the ash pit are, left to right, George Miles, labourer; his father Bob Miles, labourer, from Gloucester Street; Jack Townsend, boilerman; Eddie Stenzhorn, sawyer, from Stanford in the Vale; Jan Rogoski, labourer, from Watchfield.

1987, Eagle Motors garage at the junction of Coxwell Road and Fernham Road. It was very busy here when the traffic was passing through Faringdon but, when the by-pass was built, the trade dropped away and the site was sold for the housing development called Clocktower Place.

c.1905. The Fever Hospital consisted of three hexagonal wooden huts on the Highworth Road, about where the council yard now stands. People were isolated there when they had infectious diseases such as scarlet fever and diptheria. Mrs Elizabeth Illot is the nurse first from the left in the back row. The Matron is seated in the front.

1966, The Express Dairy in Park Road with a milk churn lorry at the milk bay. The chimney was 120 feet high and was a prominent feature in Faringdon.

Delivering the milk for the White Horse Dairy during the severe winter of 1962/3. The Dairy had to hire tractors and drivers to enable the milk deliveries to get through to the outlying villages. Sunday morning in Coxwell Road outside the Eagle Motors Garage at the Fernham Rd corner. Bill Carter driving his tractor, which he normally used on his market garden. Ann Carter (no relation) is behind him and her husband, Jimmy, is on the trailer.

1985. The interior of the Town Hall in Market Place showing its use as a public library. After the library was transferred to the Elms in Gloucester Street it was used to house the Red Cross charity shop. At one time the room was used as a subscription reading room. It also had the fire appliances and an ambulance stored underneath in the early years of this century. The Corn Market can be seen through the right-hand window.

1956. Staff of the Southern Electricity Board, Faringdon Branch, in front of Liddiard's warehouse in Swan Lane. Left to right, back row: George Cornwell; Ron Mayo; Chris Talbot; Vernon Cannons; Harry Lainchbury; Mike Buck; Don Sillence; Eric New; Bert Archer. Middle row: Les Carter; Trevor Price; Ann Bebb; Fred Morton; John Lowe; Ann Page; Jean Wordnam; Grace Archard; Donald Allnatt. Front row: Jim Larkin; Doug House; Peter Goodenough; Jim Brown; Aubrey Horn; Tony Ayres; Arthur Hobbs; Bob Hunt.

1929, Faringdon Gas Works in Canada Lane. Left to right: Ernie Walker; Harry Hancock; gas official.

1916, Mr Parker's Corn Stores, Tea Rooms and shop in Marlborough Street. Mr Parker had been there from at least 1895. The Police Station now stands on this site. Left to right: Mr Edgington; Horace Hickman; J. Parker; Frank Wheeler.

1909, the corner of London Street and Skinners Alley. Mrs H.J. Langham with her daughter Elizabeth (later Mrs Farmer of Coxwell Street) outside the family's greengrocers.

1914, Skinner's bakery in Skinners Alley, formerly called Colliers Row. Mrs Skinner holding 2 year old Norman. Legge, the delivery boy holding the bicycle, was killed in WWI. The National Trust used these premises after the bakery closed and tried to revive the old name of the street, but the Post Office would not recognise it.

SECTION THREE

Faringdon Church, House and Folly

1984 Looking north across the lawns to Faringdon House. The house was built in the mid-18th century by Henry Pye after fire had damaged the original one. Much of the material from the original was used in the new building and traces of charring can be seen on the underside of the oak flooring. Later Henry Pye had to sell the house and estate due to his and his father's debts.

The drawing shows the original Faringdon House of over 200 years earlier, a rambling Elizabethan mansion. It was twice under siege during the Civil War of 1642–1646, being a Royal Garrison and one of the last places to hold out for the king. In 1646 fighting was so fierce that the church, in a position between the Royalists in Faringdon House and the Parliamentarian guns to the east of the town, lost its steeple, the top of the tower and part of the south aisle. Two canon balls were found in the debris of the belfry when the bells were re-cast.

Folly Hill. The original Scots Pines were planted by Henry James Pye, the Poet Laureate, about 1790. In an ode for the King's birthday he referred to so many allusions of vocal groves and feathered choirs that it resulted in the nursery rhyme 'Sing a song of sixpence'. Henry Pye wrote 'Faringdon Hill' in 1774 with reference to the battle at Faringdon 'Contract the prospect now and mark more near Fair Faringdon her humble turret rear, Where once the tapering spire conspicuous grew, Till civil strife the sacred pile o'erthrew.'

The Folly Tower built in 1935 by Lord Berners. The grand opening was Nov 6th 1936 on Richard Heber-Percy's 21st birthday. It is 100 feet high and parts of six counties can be seen from its top. The hill was called the Folly long before the tower was built and was originally the site of a Celtic ring camp. In digging the foundations of the tower, some skeletons were found which were dated to the Civil War period. During WWII the tower was used as an observation post by the Home Guard. A German spy was arrested there while watching activity on the Brize Norton and Fairford aerodromes, and so the tower was bricked up. For some years after the war access was allowed but, due to vandalism, the tower was bricked up again. It was restored by Mr Heber Percy in 1983 and once a month it is opened to the public.

All Saints Church, pre-WWII, with cross-topped railings. The spire of the church was damaged in the Civil War in 1646 when the south aisle of the church was demolished. When the bells were removed to be re-cast in 1926, a broken cannon ball was found in the tower wall. In the ringing chamber is a clock of Messrs Smith & Sons of Derby, with a modern carillon machine installed in 1926, which plays a tune on the bells every three hours commencing at 6 a.m. and finishing at 9 p.m. The tunes that are played are: Sunday 'Holy, Holy, Holy'; Monday 'We love thy place O God'; Tuesday 'At the name of Jesus'; Wednesday 'God moves in a mysterious way'; Thursday 'Through the night of doubt and sorrow'; Friday 'Thy way not mine O Lord'; Saturday 'Jerusalem my happy home'. The carillon had to be wound every day by hand, by the Tower Foreman or Steeple Keeper, until the process was electrified in recent years.

1970s, the present-day Church gates being fitted by Herby Logan and Jimmy Horton, two of Russell Spinage's employees. The gates were donated by Mrs Frank Lane.

1926, re-hanging of the bells. Left to right: Eddie Hughes; ?; Tom Clark; Jack Beesly; Randal Cadel; Albert Richings (Tower foreman); Sid Cadel; Ernie Walker; M. Taylor; Frank Wheeler (clock winder); Josh Pearce; M. Webley. Sitting on the ground: Mark Haines (sextant). The bells that they had replaced had been cast by the Corrs of Aldbourne and their successors, Welis, in 1708 and 1804. The new bells came from the Loughborough Foundry and had the following inscriptions: Treble — Mears & Stainbank, Founders, London 1874 Recast 1926; Second — as treble; Third — William Buns & John Ling Churchwardens Will & Rob Cor 1708; Fourth — God Bless the Queen Recast 1926; Fifth — Recast 1926; Sixth — Mears & Stainbank, Founders, London 1874 Recast 1926 Miss Young/ Miss Jessie Young/ Miss Mary Young; Seventh — Recast 1926 Col & Mrs Ward Bennet/ Rt. Hon. Lord Berners/ Thomas Cotgrave & Enid Wilson Churchwardens. James Wells Albourne Fecit 1803; Tenor — Recast 1926 W. M.Carey Ward Vicar/ R. J. Cadel/ R. Hughes/ Churchwardens/ Cock & Henry Newman Churchwardens. R. Welis Aldbourne Fecit MDCCLXXXIIII.

1932. Bellringers outside the Vicarage. Left to right, back row: E. Walker; Rev. Carey Ward; F. Wheeler. Second row: F. H. Whipp; J. Beesley; H. Townsend; C. Pearce; E. C. Hughes; H. Edwards; T. Clarke. Seated: Bert Timms; G. Wornham; M. Pawling.

1952, April 14th, Faringdon Choir. Left to right, Adults, standing: Mr Green; W. H. Cook; John Morris; Miss Hughes; Robert Baker; Mrs Nash; Miss Obourne; ?; Miss K. Sollis; Mrs Naylor; George Cameron; Stella Proctor; Enid Naylor; ?; Canon Denis; ?; Tessa Nash; Mrs Sollis; ?; Mrs Osbourne; Bert Tame; ?; Malcolm Simpson; Les Sollis; A. B. Williams; Mr Nash. Choirboys, standing: Tony Shenton; Chris Stallard; Roy Shelton; David Ball; Mike Wheeler; Mike Sharps; John Knapp; Don Brown; Malcolm Simpson. Choirboys, sitting: Smith; Geoffrey Luckett; Nash; Smith; Michael Walker; Nick Mattingley; Michael Knapp.

SECTION FOUR

Events

To celebrate the coronation of King George V in 1911 an ox was roasted in the Market Place. Left to right (carvers & cooks): Supt. Maunders; Bob Hughes; Doc Parker, the vet; Bert Pullen; Mr Haynes; Edward Heavens; George Heavens; Tommy (Tinker) Anns.

c.1925. Raising money for the Cottage Hospital. The top of London Street with George Eastoe's grocery shop at the corner of Swan Lane. A nurse is pushing a decorated bathchair and is accompanied by a policeman and a harlequin. In the pony trap, dressed as the butcher, the baker and the candlestick maker, are Mr P. Liddiard, Mr Taylor and Thomas Burge.

THE FESTIVAL OF BRITAIN

ACTIVITIES IN FARINGDON

MAY 6th to MAY 14th 1951

A COMMITTEE of Citizens of the Town, under the Chairmanship of Mr J. V. Hale, has been formed to arrange a Programme of events for the above week. It is sincerely hoped that the events arranged will be attended by large numbers of the inhabitants in view of the fact that all profits made will be devoted to the betterment of Tucker Park, so kindly given to the Town by Walter Tucker, Esq.

The main events on each day are:

SUNDAY, MAY 6th. An open air **United Religious Service** will be held in the Market Place at 7 p.m.

MONDAY, MAY 7th. and TUESDAY, MAY 8th. The Faringdon Dramatic Society present **The Chiltern Hundreds**, by W. Douglas Home, in the Corn Exchange at 7-30 p.m. Tickets obtainable from Messrs. White Bros., Cornmarket, Faringdon.

WEDNESDAY, MAY 9th. A **Football Match** in Tucker Park. Kick-off 6-30 p.m. A Faringdon and District XI v. Swindon Town.

FRIDAY, MAY 11th. A **Grand Whist Drive** in the Corn Exchange, organised by the Faringdon R.A.O.B. at 7-30 p.m.

SUNDAY, MAY 13th. A **Concert** in the Corn Exchange, by the British Railways (Swindon) Male Voice Choir, at 7-30 p.m.

WHIT MONDAY, MAY 14th.
A **Carnival** commencing at 2 p.m. Valuable prizes. Full details and entry forms from: Mr S. G. Mills, The Limes, Bromsgrove, Faringdon.
An **Athletic Meeting** (Under A.A.A. Rules) in Tucker Park at 2-30 p.m. Open and Local Events. Excellent Prizes. All details from Mr A. Cross, Bromsgrove, Faringdon.
The **Royal Artillery Association Band, Swindon** will be in attendance and will play selections throughout the afternoon.
Side Shows. Teas and Buffet. Confetti Battle in the Market Place at 9 p.m.
Dancing in illuminated Streets 10—11 p.m.
A **Carnival Ball** in the Corn Exchange, 10 p.m.—2 a.m.

A Fine Programme as you can see has been arranged, so please come and support it and so help the Town to obtain a Playing Field worthy of its name.

1951. The three attendants to the Faringdon Beauty Queen. Left to right: Vernon James; John Doyle; Vernon Hale.

1951. Frank (Nobby) Wilkins, from Crabtree Farm, at the Carnival in Tuckers Park. He won the first prize for best heavy horse.

1953 Carnival. The Burma Star float. All eight were Burma veterans. L. to R. J. Corbishley; Fred Keogh; Pike; Jack Bryan; George Goddard; Rowland Hill; Carpenter; Bill Palmer.

CORONATION CELEBRATIONS 1953
Diary of Events

Wednesday, May 6th — Football Match in Tucker Park:
SWINDON TOWN v FARINGDON & DISTRICT. Kick-off 6.30 p.m.

Friday/Saturday, May 22nd and 23rd — Faringdon Dramatic Society present:
BEGGAR MY NEIGHBOUR in Corn Exchange, 7.30 p.m.

Whit Monday, May 25th - Carnival Day

Wednesday, May 27th — Square Dance in Corn Exchange 7 p.m. to 11 p.m.

Thursday, May 28th — Old Tyme Dance, Corn Exchange 8.30 p.m.

Friday, May 29th — Darts Tournament in Corn Exchange, 7 p.m.

Saturday, May 30th — Whist Drive in Corn Exchange 7.30 p.m.

Sunday, May 31st — United Religious Service in Market Place 7 p.m.

Tuesday, June 2nd — CORONATION DAY
- 8 a.m. to 12 noon — Roasting Pig in Market Place
- 12.15 p.m. — Distribution of Roasted Pig
- 10.30 a.m. to 4.30 p.m. — Televising of Coronation in County Grammar School for Girls. All persons 60 years and over invited
- 3 p.m. to 5 p.m. — Children's Tea Party in Market Place in two relays alternated with Cinema Show in Regent Cinema. Distribution of Coronation Mugs to children at tea tables
- 8.30 p.m. — Unveiling Ceremony of Plaque on Corn Exchange by Mr. F. Carter, with short Religious Service.

PUBLIC RELAY OF QUEEN'S SPEECH
- 9.30 p.m. to midnight — Dancing in Market Place
- 9.30 p.m. to 2 a.m. — Dance in Corn Exchange

1953 Flags and bunting decorate the streets for a Carnival in celebration of Queen Elizabeth II's Coronation. Crowds lined the whole route from the start to the venue of Tuckers Park.

1953. This impressive entry from the Saw Mills in Park Road is parked in Church Street ready for the parade to start. The giant elm was decorated with various tools of the trade and products made at the Saw Mills, such as gates, fencing, posts and brush heads. Sitting on the log were Jack Townsend and Jock Hackett.

1953. Maureen Dyer was the Carnival Queen and was attended by sisters Doris and Ada Roberts. In the front, from left to right, were Miss McKenzie and Miss Carter.

EVENTS 53

1977 Silver Jubilee celebrations. Pupils of the Infant School walked from the start of the parade in Fernham Road to Faringdon House grounds in the pouring rain. They were very proud of their prize winning entry of a crown placed on the top of a Mini car. The Headmistress, Mrs Edith Stevens, and Mrs Anita Thomas are two of the members of staff escorting the children.

1986. Some members of the Faringdon Womens Institute enjoying the Carnival fun with their 'seaside' float and at the same time supporting the swimming pool fund. Their float won third prize.

1989 Faringdon Guides 'Alice in Wonderland' float. Knave, Sarah Priest; Queen, Amanda Wright; Two of Spades, Maria Gomez; person showing her back, Jane Fox; Five of Spades, Claire Belcher; Three of Clubs, Pat Fox, Guider; Angela Carter; Dormouse, Kelly Pugh; Bird, Tina Coshall; Mad Hatter, Tara Strowger.

1911. An early traffic jam in the Market Place. London taxis, 'UNICS', with a spare tyre on the roof, had brought many foreign military attaches to Faringdon to observe Army manoeuvres. The Prime Minister, Mr Asquith, accompanied by the Duke of Connaught (his car is the white one) and many others, watched the proceedings.

1911. Army manoeuvres. Troops en route from the feeding station at Church Path farm. In the foreground is a telephone-line laying limber. Counsell's clock shows that it is late afternoon.

1931. Another occasion on which the army 'invaded' Faringdon. Store wagons moving off along Station Road (now Park Road), en route to Gough's Field (now the site of the O.B.H. Kennels) via Wicklesham Road and the bridge over the railway. One Sunday, the branch line was closed to ordinary traffic while many special trains transported everything the Army needed to Faringdon.

EVENTS 55

1989, Remembrance Day. Two standard bearers in front of the Faringdon War Memorial at the side of the Town Hall. Left: Charlie White, from Hatford, with the British Legion standard, which he carried for over 30 years. Right: Jack Bryan with the Burma Star standard, which he carried for over 40 years.

1995, St. George's Day parade by the King Alfred District Scouts and Cubs led by District Commissioners and Scout Leaders. This was the first one held after a gap of many years.

1955. On the left is Mrs H.C. Rose, president of the Faringdon W.I. and wife of C.H. Rose, solicitor. On the right is Mrs Muriel Davey, wife of Rev. Clive Davey, Vicar of Faringdon. Presenting the bouquet is Maureen Tolman at the opening of a W.I. Michaelmas sale. The proceeds were donated to the All Saints Church Restoration Fund.

Late 1960s. Enjoying a fancy dress dance at Faringdon Bowling Club. Left to right, back row: Gladys Bowerman; Mrs Bell; Milly Bryan; Jack Bryan; Jean Chapman; John Rimmer; Jane Barrett; Joan Barrett. Front row: Ruth Bryan; Albert Chapman; Brenda Rixon.

SECTION FIVE

The Market

1880. Faringdon Market Place with pens ready for market. Notice the gas lamps on the Portwell and the London Street junction. The Gas & Coke Co. were in Faringdon in 1877. The pump and drinking bowl can be plainly seen on the north side of the Portwell.

1888. It looks a sunny afternoon as shown by the auctioneer under the sun umbrella to the right of the Crown Hotel. The gentleman wearing the top hat, centre left, could be selling the baskets etc. set out around him.

May 1904, a busy Market Day with sheep, pigs, goats, chickens and geese sold in the Market Place, and horses and ponies beyond the Portwell. Note the changes in the shop fronts from the previous photograph. Still remembered today are Mr 'Minnie' Goodman and George Hughes, Town Crier, who erected the hurdles for the market and cleaned up the square at the end, a very necessary job. On the right the man with the bowler hat is Richard James.

May 1904, the Cattle Market in Church Street. A crowd of men and boys around the auctioneer's hut. Milk cattle were enclosed near the Church gates while the dry and store cattle were tethered to rings in the wall further along. Bulls were tethered on the opposite side beyond the Salutation Hotel. Note the railings on the churchyard wall which were removed during WWII to help the war effort.

THE MARKET   59

The following photographs show the new site in use in 1953.

During the early 19th century, pigs were an important part of Faringdon's economy. In 1809 no less than 4,000 hogs were slaughtered and cured in the town. In the early 1930s the Cattle Market was moved to a new site on the corner of Church Street and Coach Lane. It was not until the late 1940s that the sheep and pigs were moved to the same site. The fire engine house is in the background. Left to right: Mr Chambers, snr; ?; Frank Chambers, auctioneer; Philip Wentworth, a butcher from Stanford in the Vale and Official Grader at the Market; Dick 'Jammy' James; Guy Weaving, farmer.

George Miles leans on the wall watching Minnie Goodman pen pigs in Church Street. A policeman stood in Coach Lane every Market Day to organise the traffic, and to watch for cruel treatment and to observe movement orders for the animals.

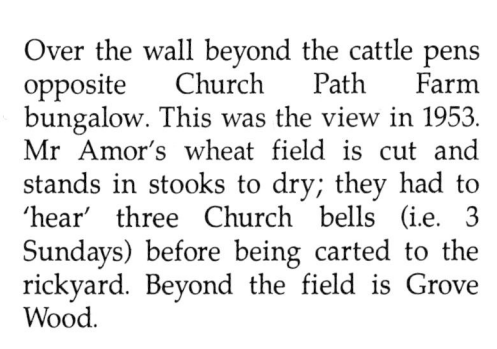

Over the wall beyond the cattle pens opposite Church Path Farm bungalow. This was the view in 1953. Mr Amor's wheat field is cut and stands in stooks to dry; they had to 'hear' three Church bells (i.e. 3 Sundays) before being carted to the rickyard. Beyond the field is Grove Wood.

SECTION SIX

Personalities

Michael Giannadrea at the Church gates after attending a wedding. He fought in WWI for Italy and came to this country in 1919, obtaining a job with Halls Brewery, Oxford. He sent for his family to join him when he was offered the position of licensee of the Duke of York pub on the corner of Gravel Walk and Coxwell Street. He had a large allotment on the Sands where he grew vegetables which his wife sold on the steps of the pub. She always wore a spotless white apron and a white scarf on her head. Giannadrea designed his own icecream wagon which was then built for him by Mr A. Baker. Giannadrea used to attend local fêtes and go round the villages with his pony pulling the wagon selling his homemade icecream. He became Faringdon's oldest and longest serving licensee.

PERSONALITIES   61

1981 Fernham Parish Meeting. Jim and Ruth Brown. The photograph was taken at an exhibition of 'Country Life through the Ages' organised by Jim and Ruth to raise money for Fernham Church. The butter churn and steam bath (behind) came from Coleshill House and were loaned by the National Trust. Jim was born at Challow Station in 1932 and went to Goosey School. He became an apprentice electrician at Wantage at the age of 14. He finished his apprenticeship with the S. E. B. in Faringdon and then was called up for National Service. He spent most of that time in Germany serving with the R. A. F. on Super Sabres doing electrical work. He was a very keen motor cyclist and shared his enthusiasm with his wife Ruth whom he married at Eaton Hastings in 1957. Jim was also a keen sailor and spent a lot of time on Faringdon Lake and Buscot Park reservoir in a sailing dinghy. He helped his brother in law to build two boats. Jim's enthusiasm for collecting photographs began when the county boundaries were changed in 1974 and he now has a collection of about 4,000. He started to show some of the slides in a show he called 'Nostalgia Evening' and this has grown in popularity over the years. He is always willing to receive copies of 'new' photographs to add to his collection. Jim also serves on the Fernham Parish Council and was, for a long time, a governor of Longcot School. He belongs to the British Heart Foundation and Faringdon & District Historical Society. At Christmas he makes an excellent Father Christmas, the children often asking if his beard is real and giving it a big tug. Ruth was born at Buscot Park Estate in 1934 and went to Faringdon School, where she was head girl. She left school at fifteen and went to work as a dental nurse at the practice of Kerr and Vine. She continued to work there until her two children arrived. Jim and Ruth also have four grandchildren. They have lived at their house, for which they drew up the plans, at Fernham, for 36 years. Ruth helps Jim with his photographs and, when he is giving a slide show, she takes notes of any new information. They both enjoy gardening and grow all their own vegetables.

Left to right: John Carter; Jim Cave, manager of Carter's store for many years; Norman Carter.

John was born in 1937 and Norman in 1938. They were the sons of Cyril John Carter who owned Carter's, the grocery store, in Marlborough Street. The Carter family had been associated with the business since 1848. Cyril Carter, with his sisters Kathleen and Phyllis, took control of the business in 1925, the sisters leaving to take over Lay's shop in the Market Place when Cyril married. John and Norman assumed control of the business, with their mother, when Cyril became ill in 1953. In the same year they purchased the butcher's business of Taylor & Sons at 6, Cornmarket and John managed that side of the affairs. In 1962 the main shop was given a face lift and made into a self-service store. The shop was further enlarged in 1966/67. The Carter brothers purchased the garden of the Red Lion public house, again enlarging the floor space of the store, and gaining access to the town car park in Southampton Street. In 1975 the centre of the store and the warehouse were demolished and rebuilt, thus expanding the store to 7,500 sq. ft. In the years that followed John and Norman purchased both Nos. 5 and 7 Marlborough Street, and the store was enlarged yet again. In 1986 Carter's was one of the first grocery shops in the United Kingdom to use scanning at the exit tills. In that same year the remainder of 5 Marlborough Street was incorporated into the store as a new wine department. In 1996 the Carter brothers sold the store to Budgens.

Percival Frank White was born in 1920. He had an elder brother, Henry, who had been born two years earlier. Their parents were Frank and Ruth White who ran a hairdresser, tobacconist and stationery shop in the Corn Market. This business had been started by Percival's great grandfather, George, around 1820 and continued by his grandfather, Henry. Percival left school at the age of 14 years and joined his parents in the shop. His uncle, Percival Henry White, was also a hairdresser in the business and he declared that there couldn't be two people of the same name working there. He told young Percival that he would be called Bill and from then on this was the name that everyone knew him by. During the World War II, Bill joined the 5th Berkshire Home Guard Battalion as a despatch rider.

The following are the names of the men in the battalion. **Co. Commander**: Major P. Colwell. **2nd Lt.**: Capt. N. Fletcher. **Transport Officer**: Lt. T. Clare. **Platoon Commander**: Lt. P. F. White. **M.V.O.** Lt. Sir Hugh Gurney. **Medical Officer**: Capt. G. Stenhouse. **Q.M.S.**: L. Sollis. **Sergeants**: H. Edmonds; T. Filgate; V. Tytherleigh; W. Packer; J. Imms; E. Head; A. King. **Corporals**: B. Tame; J. Pook; E. Foard; J. Smith. **Lance Corporals**: J. Barnes; F. Edwards; A. Seary; J. Nichol. **Privates**: W. Ayres; A. Archer; W. Amor; K. Arnold; A. Barrett; R. Berry; E. Betterton; R. Bolter; A. Carpenter; W. Davis; K. Day; R. Davis; T. Emery; S. Fox; B. Fisher; W. Foard; F. Freeguard; S. Gills; L. Gorton; J. Gilmore; H. Goldstick; R. Greenaway; E. Grainger; W. Hearing; C. Head; S. Harris; R. Haskins; L. Hopkins; P. Hunt; M. Harris; D. Harris; H. Higginbotham; C. Harris; C. Jupe; R. Large; J. Morbey; H. Margetts; S. Nash; R. Niker; C. Pearce; C. Peaty; L. Pauling; C. Pill; T. Preston; A. Read; W. Robinson; F. Rees; G. Rich; A. Rixon; A. Saunders; H. Sellwood; B. Sharpes; N. Skinner; L. Smith; J. Sollis; F. Townsend; R. Wheeler; W. Willis; F. Whiting; C. Winney; S. Young. **Past Members Faringdon Platoon**: Lt. W. Tucker; Lt. C. McDonald; Sgt. C. Button; Q.M.S. J. Wright; Sgt. G. Ibbetson; Cpl. W. Belcher. **Privates**: V. Adams; E. Airs; C. Alder; F. Bowerman; A. Bowman; L. Buzwell; M. Calvert; A. Carpenter; C. Chinn; L. Coles; L. Cook; P. Cox; A. Edgington; F. Edwards; W. Freeguard; C. Gerring; H. Golding; B. Gosling; W. Gover; T. Griffiths; W. Hill; F. Holmes; F. Hoskins; F. Hughes; M. Ibbetson; A. Jackson; E. James; K. Kerr; R. Laslett; T. Lloyd; H. Loder; T. Luckett; W. Luckett; A. Manning; S. Marchant; Matthias; E. Moynes; T. Nelson; R. Nikolson; R. Nunn; T. O'Connell; A. Page; H. Page; A. Palmer (killed in action); C. Paul; C. Roberts; W. Robinson; W. Rudgard; V. Saunders; F. Smith; H. Smith; T. Stepp; R. Stickley (killed in action); F. Strong; D. Weber; J. Williams; C. Willis.

Gwendoline Tanner was born at Cirencester in 1923 and Bill met her when his brother was courting her sister, Joyce. Bill, Henry and Joyce had been to a car rally and on the way back they had a slight accident with the car so it was decided to take Joyce back home first. Bill asked her if there was another one at home like her, Joyce replied that there was her young sister Gwen. Joyce and Gwen joined the Armed Forces during the war and, as the romance blossomed between her and Bill, Gwen applied to transfer to the W.R.N.S. based in Faringdon. The sisters were married on the same day at Faringdon in 1944, Joyce to Don Slingsby and Gwen to Bill. Bill liked to play tennis and helped to rejuvenate the Tennis Club. He was an enthusiastic supporter for a swimming pool in the Corn Exchange but unfortunately it failed to materialise. He also became interested in local politics, serving on the Council for about 30 years, being mayor for four years and becoming so well known that he was often called 'Mr. Faringdon'. Bill died on 1st September 1996 aged 76 years

Jack Bryan was born on 15th July 1917 at Westbrook Cottages, Gravel Walk to Fred and Alice Bryan. In 1919, when his twin sisters, Gill and Joan, were born, they were living in a cottage in Lechlade Road opposite the 'Duke of Wellington'. He started school firstly in the Congregational Chapel School room in 1922, then moved to Southampton Street Infants school and finally to the British School in Lechlade Road. He left school in 1931 for his first job as grocer's boy at Chamberlain's in London Street. In May 1939 with war looming, he joined the Territorial Army and in September was called up and served in the Royal Berkshire Regiment throughout the war. He survived Dunkirk and later went to Burma, finally arriving home on Boxing Day 1945. After being demobbed his next job was at the Co-op grocer's in Marlborough Street where he stayed for 8 years. This was followed by 4 years as a postman until he went to work at Pressed Steel (Rover) in Swindon where he worked for 20 years until his retirement in 1977 due to ill health. Jack has many interests, he played football and was a founder member of the Thursday Football Club in 1936 and was secretary for the Memorial Competition for 28 years. He enjoyed playing cricket, watching tennis and athletics. His enthusiasm for watching athletics has taken him to many parts of the United Kingdom and the world, including going to the Olympics. He was also a Parish Councillor for some years. For 40 years Jack carried the Burma Star standard and is a stalwart member of the Association and also of the Royal British Legion. Jack, who is now using an invalid scooter, is a familiar figure around Faringdon and is always ready to share his memories of old Faringdonians and of times gone by. Milly Bryan was born at Shellingford in 1924, the daughter of Mr and Mrs George Mitchell. She attended school in Faringdon. She often used to help her father deliver the shoes that he had repaired, to his customers. On 6th September 1947 she married Jack Bryan at Shellingford and their first home was in Gravel Walk. In 1953 they moved to Bennett Road, followed by a home in Goodlake Avenue and finally to a flat in the Eagles. They have two sons and a daughter and nine grandchildren. After her marriage to Jack, she stayed at home to look after her family, only going back to work when they had grown up. She worked for 38 years at Carter's grocery store where she was a familiar figure at the kiosk selling tobacco items. She retired at the age of 73 to continue with her favourite hobby of researching her family history. In July 1997 Jack and Milly attended the Buckingham Palace Garden Party for the occasion of the Queen and Prince Philip's Golden Wedding celebrations. They celebrated their own Golden Wedding with a party at the Faringdon Bowling Club.

PERSONALITIES 65

Bromsgrove Farm House garden. The wedding of Harry Watts and Winnie Cox. The best man was Harry Abel and bridesmaid, far left, Eva Abel. The bride's mother is seated on the right and her father at bride's elbow. Mr and Mrs Albert Cox are next to the father. The lady seated on the extreme left is thought to be Mrs Cox of Longcot, the bride's grandmother. The man with the beard at the centre back is Mr Colin Sell and on his left Mr Cox, the bride's brother, next to his nurse.

SECTION SEVEN

Public Houses

It has been alleged that Rosa May James wrote the following for her son in 1896 to show how many pubs there were in Faringdon.

'Driving into the town of Faringdon this morning I was delighted to find an old and valued friend *The Duke of Wellington* and having shaken hands with him by way of *Salutation* we proceded down Glos'ter St escorted by the *Volunteer* and made the best of our way to *Marlborough Arms*. We had just seated ourselves for a drink when the Landlord informed us that the *Angel* had seen the *Crown* knocked out of the *Queens Arms* by the *Duke of York*. Determined to see if such a thing was true we started away to Coxwell St where we met the *Gardener* with the *Wheatsheaf* in his arms just preparing to feed the *Swan*. He told us he had never heard of such a thing but since our arrival in town there has been a desperate fight between the *Red Lion* and the *Eagle* and that the eagle was at the top of the street and the lion was chasing the *White Hart* all round the *Folly*. Off we set again and getting to the Market Place we were alarmed at the tolling of the *Bell*. Enquiring what was the matter we were told that the *Tap* had been stopped and the old *Bull* had kicked the *Star* over into the *Bakers Arms*.'

The following are some of the pubs mentioned above.

The Duke of Wellington, Lechlade Road.

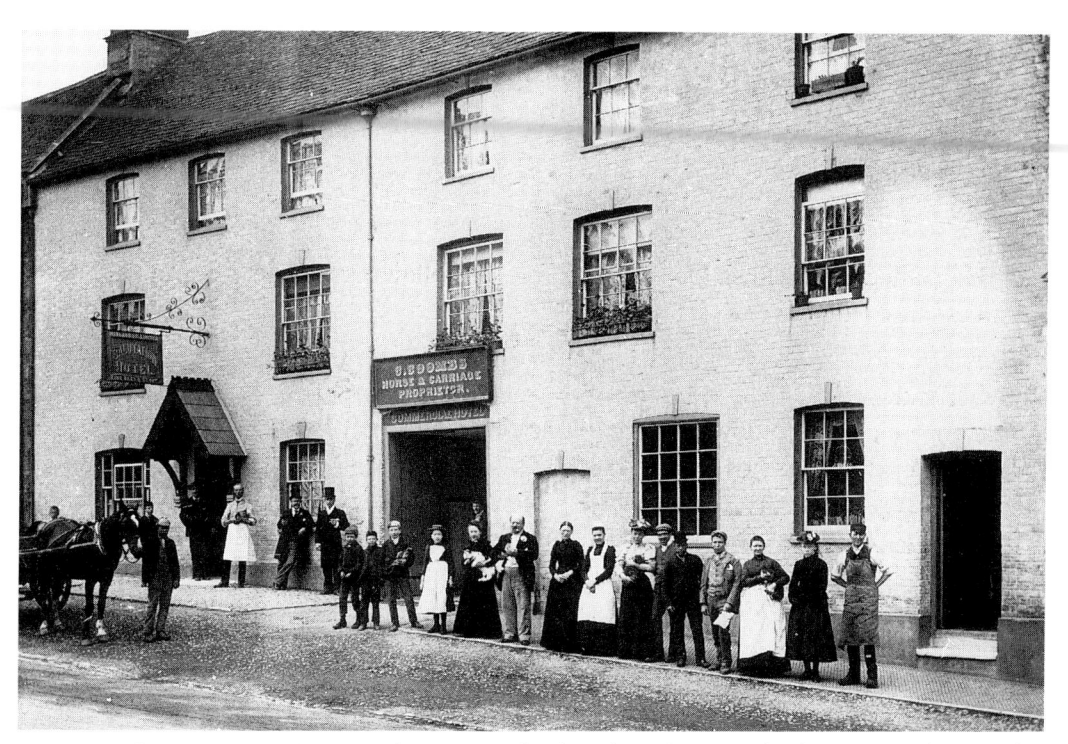

c.1880s. Salutation Hotel, Church Street. The hotel took over the house on the Market Place, owned by Mr Pethers, at a later date (1911). This was a coaching inn, the entrance visible in the middle of the picture. The coach and horses used to go through the entrance into a yard and then exit into the Market Place between Mr Pether's house and Crowdy & Rose. The left-hand side of the hotel was later a doctors' surgery. The hotel required numerous staff to run it and here are some of them photographed with mine host. The landlord is dressed in a frock coat and his wife is next to him holding a dog in her arms.

1953. The Volunteer Inn, Gloucester Street.

1953. The Market Place. In the background is the Crown Hotel. This was the chief inn in Faringdon as far back as 1681 when Thomas Baskerville visited the town. Note the arch for the entry of horses and coaches. There were stables behind the inn for the horses. The County Court held monthly sessions in the Crown until it moved to the Court in Coach Lane. The Crown was also used as an Excise Office. The adjacent building used to be part of the Crown and was called the Angel Inn, this was where the drivers and labourers drank whilst their 'betters' patronised the Crown Inn. On the side of this building can be seen the doorways to the Angel and also to the old Post Office which was there until the new Post Office was built in Marlborough Street. In the foreground on the left is Jack Davis from Langford's coalyard in Bromsgrove, and the man holding the bike is Arthur (Stoker) Edgington. The man on the right, in breeches, is Stanley Liddiard from Liddiard's shop. Just in front of the Portwell is Burtwell & Drew's Raleigh three-wheeler van.

1953. The Duke of York Inn at the corner of Coxwell St. and Gravel Walk, licensee Michael Giannadrea. On the other side of Gravel Walk can be seen Boffin's butcher's shop with the public weighbridge in front. Crossing the junction is Cadel's milk churn lorry en route to the Express Dairy. Mervyn Carter, butcher's boy, is on his delivery bike. On the right, the iron railings enclose Mr Absolom's outfitter's shop in Station Road.

PUBLIC HOUSES 69

1953. The Gardeners Arms, Coxwell Street, now a private house. Further up the road are The Queens Arms and the Eagle.

1953. The Wheatsheaf, London Street. The stables were at the rear of the pub so the horse had to be taken down a narrow passage to reach them. The landlord was Mr Chandler who had been a cowboy in the U.S.A. and decorated the bar with his memorabilia of those days.

The Swan, Christopher Square.

The Red Lion, Corn Market. The end of the building shows where Mr Taylor's fish shop was demolished to create the site for the Post Office.

c.1910. The Eagle, Coxwell Street. The Queens Arms (was the Pink Elephant) is half way down on the left. The Gardeners Arms is further down the road. The man on the horse is the local doctor, Dr. Kennard, accompanied by his faithful dog. This dog stayed with the horse whilst the doctor was making his calls, and allowed no one to approach the horse. Note how high the pavements are from the unmade road. Children used to sit on the pavement and dangle their legs over the edge. The children in the picture are dressed in the costume of the day. Note the breeches and caps worn by the boys and the gleaming white apron and hat worn by the girl on the left.

1953. The White Hart, Gravel Walk, now converted to flats. Ann's garage is on the right (now the re-built Peugeot showroom).

1953. The Folly, London Street.

1953. The Bell Inn, Market Place, on the right, was once a tenement of Beaulieu Abbey and later a coaching inn with stables at the back. The buildings on London Street are occupied by Noel Wilkes' ladies and gents outfitters; Mr Thair's boot and shoe shop; W.H. Smith's paper shop; Shenton's sweet shop; a private house; Chamberlain's grocery shop.

Early 1900s, London Street. The Bull is on the right and the Star on the left.

The Bakers Arms in Ferndale Street, also known as Back Street. This street used to be called Union Street because Faringdon Poor Law Union, commonly known as the Workhouse, was situated there. The Union building was demolished in 1968 and is now the site of Brackendale and the Pitts Estate.

SECTION EIGHT

Schools

1938, Faringdon County Senior School. Left to right, back row: Enid Burbidge; Joyce Warren; Phyllis Baily; ?; June Lewis; Betty Underwood; Marjorie Parker; Mary Hudson; Jean Pauling; Jean Hill; Doreen Page; Olive Higgins; June Jackson; Rene Dowell; Betty Stanton; Rosemary White; Margaret Norton; Ida Warner; Freda Willis. Second row: Percy Blundy; ?; Billy Hinchcliffe; Harry Thomas; Frank Large; Leslie Bunce; Fred Stone; Jack Prior; Holcombe; Bill Pett; Jack Fox; Mary Stallard; Joan Goodenough; Mary Underwood; Jean Hunt; Joan Bunce; Iris Bailey; Annie Hallett; Milly Mitchell; Joyce Bowley; ?. Third row: John Moody; ?; Fred Giannadrea; Ken Freeman; ?; Len Busby; Harold Clarke; Brian Packer; Cyril Roberts. Fourth row: Archie Debank; Dennis Mildenhall; Jim Fox; Ernie Packford; ?; Janet Preston; Ruby Goodall; Betty Burch; Phyllis Bailey. Front row: Des Ball; Harold Hambidge; ?; ?; ?; Cyril Wirdnam; ?; Betty Rouse; Kathleen Iles; Betty Butler; Peggy Mildenhall; Joan Strong; Madge Richens; Jean Packer.

Late 1920s/early 1930s, New Girls School. The Infants School was a separate building beyond this. Later, the gap was filled by a large school hall joining the two schools together. The Infants School then moved to the present site in Lechlade Road and the Southampton Street School became Faringdon Secondary Modern School.

Mid-1950s. High School for Girls, Gloucester Street (The Elms). Headmistresses of the school were Miss Bartlett, Miss A. H. Moore, Miss Towns.

74 CHANGING FACES OF FARINGDON

The High School for Girls, The Elms, Gloucester Street. Inside the Chemistry Laboratory. In the foreground: Naomi Hamlin. Behind, right to left: Dorinda Knapp; Diane Wilson; ?; Ann Jones(?) from Puzey.

1955. Faringdon Senior School staff, Southampton Street. Left to right, back row: Mr Hodson (Maths); Mr Venn; Alan Anthony; Robert Henry; ?; ?; George Young. Middle row: ?; Mrs Smith; ?; Mr Gibson (Gardening); Mrs Mary Jenn (Secretary); Gordon Archard; ?; Mary Firman; Betty Lilley. Front row: Barbara Richings (Domestic Science); Arthur Holifield (Art); Mrs Farmer (Deputy Head/Needlework); Arnold Willes (Headmaster); Roland Hill (Deputy Head); Kathleen Allanson (P.E.); Miss Reece (later Mrs Holifield)

SCHOOLS 75

Faringdon Secondary Modern School. Sixth Form on a visit to Mr Carter's market garden in Fernham Road.

Faringdon Secondary Modern School Sports Day prize-giving in Southampton Street. Left to right: Rev. Davey; John Davies, headmaster; Jack Hale, governor; Mr Tunnicliffe, governor.

76 CHANGING FACES OF FARINGDON

1960s, Tollington School. First Year pupils leaving the school at the end of the day. Only these pupils were at the school as the rest of the school building was unfinished.

1964. Planting a commemorative tree at the official opening of Tollington School. The planting site was in the main entrance paved area adjacent to the administrative block. Left to right: Lady Angela Walker from Ringdale Manor, Fernham; John Davies, headmaster from Fernham Road; ?; Jack Hale, governor and stationmaster from Market Place; John Hunt of Everest fame; Fred (Skimmy) Hughes, groundsman from Ferndale Street.

SCHOOLS 77

c.1920, Faringdon Girls School, London Street. Left to right, back row: Kathleen Bunting; Louie Townsend; Mary Hill (or Belcher); Violet Haynes; Gus Parker; Bella Turner; Vera Seary; Lally Willis; ?. Second row: Dora Belcher; — Jackson; Phyllis Church; — Belcher; Kath Edmonds; Violet Dixey; — Monk; Ivy Burson; Doris Huntley?. Third row: ?; Win Tilling; Doris Nelson; Dora Stevens; ?; — Debank; Mona Clark; ?; Nelna Goodenough. Front row: Phyllis Huntley; Rose Platt; Nellie Palmer; Bess Perry; Mary Edgington.

1927, Faringdon Girls School, Southampton Street. Left to right, back row: ?; Daisy Whiting; ?; ?; Elsie Pill; ?; ?; — Palmer; ?; ?. Second row: ?; Laura Whipp; Kath Smith; ?; Beryl Arlott; ?; ?; Mary Vaughan; — Panting; Phyllis Goodall; ?. Third row: ?; — Palmer; Violet Edgington; Milly Deane; ?; ?; ?; Renee Smith; Joan Bryan. Front row: ?; ?; Dorothy Betterton; ?; Gillian Bryan.

1948, Secondary School, Southampton Street, Class 2A. Left to right, back row: Dick Holcombe; Tom Osbourne; John Reason; Sheila Sargent; Joan Ash; Dorothy Phillips; Mary Biles; Joe Smith; Tony Ayres; Bruce Wilson. Middle row: Fred Timms; Derick Mosely; ?; Robin King; Ted Whiting; Phillip Merritt; ?; Alec Titcomb; Leo Curley; John Jones; Arthur Stubbs. Front row: Sheila Burgess; Beryl Harris; Ann Cornish; Ann Peck; Ann Durham; Muriel Clements; Daphne Smith; Phylis Rudman; Josephine Gaule; Lucy Goddard; Emily Fitchett; ?.

1936, Boys C of E School, Stanford Road.

1937. Faringdon Senior School staff at the opening of the school in Southampton Street. There were approximately 87 pupils from Faringdon and Uffington. It was the first time that senior boys and girls had attended the same school. Left to right, back row: Mr Austen (Craft and Woodwork); Joyce Tollington (Sewing and Cookery); Mr Roland Hill (French, Science, Sports and General form master). Front row: Miss Woodward; Mr Willes (Headmaster); Miss Grace Godwin (General class mistress).

1933/4/5, Southampton Street Girls School. Left to right, back row: Queenie Cross; Marjorie Emmans; Eileen Willis; Eileen Tucker; Molly Humphries; Vera Packer. Second row: Violet Goodman; Ivy Goodman; Dorothy Page; – Lee; Freda Willis; Mary Palmer; Mary Moore; Marjorie Parker; Gwen Parker; Molly Cannons; Kitty Smith. Third row: ?; Rosemary Spackman; ?; Marjorie Frankam; Edith or Hilda Hibberd; Vera Church; Kathleen Geary; Ann Spackman; Edith Clack; Florrie Page. Front row: Barbara –; Grace Gray; Betty Butler; Doreen Rogers; Hilda or Edith Hibberd; Phyllis Weaving; Ruth Moore.

1972. Interschools Six a Side Football Competition. Winners Faringdon Junior School 'A' Team. Left to right, back row: Michael Mills; Scott Hunter; ?; ?. Front row: Bobby Pearce; Dennis Organ; Gary Newman.

1953. Lechlade Road showing the British School built in 1872 for 177 pupils where boys and girls, aged from 7 to 14 years, attended. One of the best remembered head teachers was Henry Proctor. Today it is the County Infants School.

SCHOOLS 81

c.1920. Infants School, Lechlade Road. Left to right, back row: ?; — Langham; Sid Ford; Wally Herring; Gerald Druet; ?; ?; George Rogers; ?; ?; Jack Page. Second row: ?; ?; Betty Willis; Flossie Smith; Nellie Osborne; ?; Nancy Long; ?; ?; — Ponting; — Whiting. Front row: ?; Jack Smith; Bert Rixon; ?; Jim Goodenough; Norman Loder; Bill Elbrow.

1925. Faringdon Infants School, Southampton Street, Class I. Left to right, back row: John Lane; Kath Smith; Jack Bryan; — Clanfield; Laura Whipp; David Boffin; — Brooks; — Stewart; Nancy Willis; Miss Wright. Middle row: Gladys Bowerman; Zena Bowerman; Eric Pauling; — Hunt; Billy Bath; Vic Purbrick; Marjorie Page; Horace Turner. Front row: Ernie Higginbothom; — Goodman?; Daisy Goodman; Bert Talbot; Len Gorton.

SECTION NINE

Societies and Sports

1903. Faringdon Military Band playing for a garden party at Faringdon House. Left to right, back row: F. Newman; G. Vickery; – Baker; A. Cobden; H. Burge; P. White; R. Smith; C. Mate; – Howarth; C. Alder. Front row: – Winkle; S. Burge; A. Taylor; W. Ballard; W. Foard, bandmaster; A. Austin; W. Walker; E. May, jnr.; E. May snr. **Side Drummer**: W. Gosling. **Big drum**: A. Gosling.

William Rabbetts Foard was born in 1851 in Woolstone. He became a grocer and a local Methodist preacher in Faringdon. In the 1890s, he formed the Faringdon Military Band and it continued successfully until the outbreak of World War I. After the war, he founded a string quartet and a Quadrille Band.

SOCIETIES AND SPORTS

1927. Whit Monday Sports on the sports field by the Wicklesham Road (Park Road filling station is now on the site). The race was across the field. The men had to mount their horses, race across the field, dismount, loop the reins over their shoulders, get their ladies into the wheelbarrow and trundle them back across the field. If a lady fell out, or if a horse was released, they had to go back to the start. Peter Liddiard's fiancee was supposed to take part but was taken ill with appendicitis, so her sister deputised for her. Peter farmed at Steeds Farm, Great Coxwell, which is now held by his grandson Andrew Liddiard.

Faringdon Swimming Baths. D. Bowerman; E. Fletcher; E. Fletcher; L. Fletcher. It was on the site close to Acorn Garage opposite Oriel Cottages. The pool was unheated, open to the elements and occupied by newts and frogs. Nevertheless many learned to swim here. The school children were taken by classes to the pool. Faringdon now has a brand new 25 metre pool in part of the Leisure Centre in Fernham Road.

The Burma Star Association was formed in Faringdon District in 1953. Fred Keogh, George Goddard and Jack Bryan attended the first meeting. The Association has gone from strength to strength and has been supported by friends and families who have enjoyed many dinner dances of up to 150 people. The group still functions but on a smaller scale, mainly due to the ageing membership. They meet once a month and have an annual luncheon, a Christmas luncheon and other social events such as an outing to Earls Court for a military tattoo. Members and their wives went to London for the 50th anniversary celebrations, a day enjoyed by all. The Annual Reunion in the Albert Hall has now been discontinued, again owing to the age of members. However the annual parade at the Whitehall Cenotaph is still held, although there are many wheelchairs in evidence now.

1978. Left to right, standing: Charlie Hicks; Joe Maynard; Alfie Mildenhall; Jack Beasley; George Dyer; Dougie Robbins; Bob Cherry; Charlie Hambidge; Jack Bryan; Charlie Pratt; Jim Cave; Fred Bastin; George Goddard; Ian Goodman; Cyril Veall; 'Tug' Wilson; Ron Buckett. Front row: Rowland Hill; Major General Abrahams; Brigadier Calvert (Mad Mike); Arthur Edgington.

1974. The 1st Faringdon Brownies attending a Thinking Day service. Left to right: R. Claire Harrison; Helen Toombs; Emma Thompson; Yvonne Hunt; Lynn Mander; Angela Norton.

Faringdon Bowling Club v Berkshire Representative Team. At this time the Bowling Club was considered an élite club mainly for business men. It was situated in Southampton Street next to the Tennis Club and White Horse Dairy (Camerons). Faringdon was in desperate need of a by-pass and it was planned to build it from Coxwell Street through Bromsgrove, taking in the top of Southampton Street and out to the Stanford Road. This prompted the decision to move the Bowling Club to Gravel Walk on land owned by Fred Carter, an ideal site. It is still a thriving Bowls Club but nowadays it is enjoyed by larger circle of people.

Left to right, back row: ?; F. Wilson; ?; ?; ?; ?; T. Hicks; L. Gough; ?; ?; ?; G. Cameron; K. Baker. Middle row: P. Coombes; G. Reason; ?; F. Carter; C. Smith; A. Baker; — Campbell-Dykes; ?; ?; ?; J. Thomas. Front row: F. Thair; B. Brighton; B. Tame; R. Bartlett; T. Hogan; ?; F. Austen; P. Tilling.

1977. Junior School, Lechlade Road, Netball team. Left to right: Christine Wood; Lynn Mander; Tracey Clarke; Vivien Laws; Alison Newman; Carol Haste.

1930–31. Faringdon Council School, Lechlade Road (the present day Infant School). Left to right, back row: Mr P.Tidyman; Eric Pauling; Ken Webb; Douglas Perkins; Bill Carter; 'Gaffer' Hamlin. Middle row: Jim Panting; Leslie Wright; Jack Bryan; Tony Packer; Gilbert Whiting.
Front row: Lennie Stallard; Eric Gee. Many pupils were taught by Mr Tidyman, a strict disciplinarian but very popular. He took his pupils to visit football matches and sports events. Highlights came at the Fairford Carnival when winning the boys' tug-o-war for several years in a row. They were also coached by P.C. Hawkins who trained the boys in Baker's field by letting them pull against a tree.

May 1993. Cutting the tape on the re-opening of the Tennis Club courts. Left to right, at the net: Robin Liddiard; Ron Liddiard; Alan Elbourn (Chairman). The land in Southampton Street, on which the club stands, was leased for 500 years to the Liddiard family in 1740. In 1925 George E. Liddiard leased it to the Tennis Club for the remaining 315 years. He appointed himself, Frank Lane and Walter Tucker as Trustees. In 1940, by which time Mr Liddiard had died, seven more Trustees were appointed. The Club's membership has fluctuated over the years but in the 1950s Bill White, Henry Hicks and their families, rejuvenated it and now it has more than 100 members aged from 8 to 70 years. In 1993 the Water Board dug a deep trench to install a new sewer from the Bellway estate. This meant that the courts had to be re-surfaced and the courts were out of use for almost five months. Unfortunately, within two weeks of the re-opening, Faringdon experienced a cloud burst and the courts were flooded half-way up the nets. There are three hard all-weather courts on which play continues all through the year.

SOCIETIES AND SPORTS

1947. Faringdon, Boxing Day Meet. In the late 18th and early 19th centuries the Old Berks Hunt territory stretched from beyond Fairford to Thame and Stokenchurch. In 1845 it was decided to separate the Vale of the White Horse Hunt and the Old Berks Hunt by splitting their territories at the R. Thames and the R. Cole. The country to the south of the Thames and to the east of the Cole would be hunted by the Old Berks and the opposite sides of the rivers by the Vale of the White Horse Hunt. In 1871 a fox ran through part of Faringdon and, jumping through a window at the home of James Clarke, Westbrook Villa in Bromsgrove, took shelter beneath a hearth rug in the front room. It was later caught and destroyed. Two outbreaks of rabies occurred in 1885 and most of the pack of hounds had to be destroyed.

The Dramatic Society was formed in 1948 from an Evening Class run by Bill Reeves. The first performances were in the Corn Exchange, while the rehearsals were held in the Meeting House opposite the Duke of Wellington and sets were built in garages and back gardens. In 1952 the Society was able to rent an old Nissen hut on the old Marines Camp (now Marines Drive and Town End Road). The members of the society converted the building into the Little Theatre (see picture above). The hut had been built by the Royal Marine Engineers during WWII and had been used as a cinema and afterwards as a store shed. The members did all the conversion themselves, repairing the roof, re-wiring, making theatre curtains, etc. The seats were bought for 3 shillings each from the American Base at Brize Norton. The first production was 'The Late Christopher Bean' by Emlyn Williams and the official opening was performed by Lord Faringdon. The Society produced over 50 plays in the theatre and remained there until about 1972 when the site was incorporated into a housing estate. After leaving the hut they put on plays in many local village halls and presented pageants in Faringdon Church. In 1978 they moved into the newly built theatre in the Community Centre where they produced a great number and variety of plays and pantomimes. There have been numerous helpers 'behind the scenes' and over three hundred performers 'out in front'. Today they are producing their plays in the Corn Exchange, the theatre in the Community Centre and Faringdon School hall.

June 1952. Members of the Faringdon and District Dramatic Society. Left to right, back row: ?; Bob Drew; ?; Doris Willis; Tony Ansell; Mr Gregson; Pat Purcell; Bill Carter; Betty and Arthur Peck (administrators from the Western Players); ?. Front row: Bill and Nancy Reeves; Eileen Drew; George Young; Kathleen Allanson; Cyril Wordnam; Margaret Bolton; Arthur Probert.

1939. Faringdon Thursday team at Oxford. Left to right, back row: Bernard Cook; Pete Wilkins; Jack Bryan; Leslie Wright; John Purbrick; Jack Benford; referee. Front row: Clarence Chambers; Maurice Gosling; Johnny Alder; Ronnie Stevens; Sid Peaty. Faringdon won 7–2. The team was formed in 1936 to cater for men who worked in shops when the early closing day was on a Thursday. The first meeting took place in Frank Mortimer's home at the rear of Chamberlain's. Cyril Vincent was its first secretary. The team joined the Oxfordshire Thursday League and played until the outbreak of the war. Afterwards it was decided that the money remaining in the bank would be used to run a Football Competition on the same lines as the defunct Hospital Cup and call it the Faringdon Thursday Memorial Cup Competition. Proceeds were donated towards the building of the new Tucker Park pavilion. This was dedicated on Thursday 26th September 1963 by the Rev. John Cook, a former player, to the memory of the players who died in the 1939–45 war. Their names are inscribed on a brass plate in the pavilion, with another dedicated to past presidents and vice-presidents. (See below.)

SOCIETIES AND SPORTS 89

1963. Dedication of the Pavilion. Left to right: Jim Angless; Jack Bryan.

This Pavilion was erected in memory of those comrades of the Thursday Football Club who fell in the 1939-45 War.
"Lest we forget"

LESLIE WRIGHT	RONALD STEVENS
HAROLD PRIESTMAN	GILBERT WHITING
ARTHUR MERCER	MICHAEL TUCKER

Also in memory of Dr J B Pulling, President and Benefactor.

DEDICATED TO THE MEMORY OF

Dr J B Pulling (President 1951-59) Bernard W Cook Esq. (President 1959-70) G R Davis Esq. (President 1970-1994)

L Sollis Esq. K Knox Esq. M Gosling Esq. J Angless Esq.
H R Bartlett Esq.

Pre-1939, Faringdon Town F.C. played on Swindon Town ground. Left to right, back row: Charlie Clements; Sid Rouse; Jack Arlidge; Eric Gee; Dick Cox (goalkeeper); Harry Gills; Jack Ward (chairman); Basil Sharps (reserve). Front row: Jack Adams (trainer); Len Gorton; Cyril Harris (Buckle); Sid Peaty; Elisha Hayes; Michael Tucker.

April 8th 1950. Faringdon Town Football Club at Abingdon when they were beaten by Hanney in the North Berks Cup. Left to right, back row: Jack Smith; Don Sillence; Ron Jackson; Vic Wilson; John Moody; Jack Gleave; Ted Mattingley. Front row: Ron (Bonzo) Imms; Fred (Skimmy) Hughes; Frank Hawkins; Ken Knox; Jack Cathcart.

Buffs outing to Southsea in Tommy Clare's coach. Left to right: Tommy Woods; ?; Jack Davis (cycle shop); — Cratchley; Harry Allway; Fred Law; Sid Peaty; coach driver; Bill Goodenough; Arthur Allnat; Eddie Peaty; Fred Townsend; Fred Birch; Bernis Gerring; Harry Hancock; Fred Bowerman; Harold Mills; Mr Hancock snr.; ?; ?; Geo Hall(?); Fred Peaty; Geo. Sollis; Bill Hunt; Jack Stevens; Frankie Wright; Bill Tombs; Fred Walker; Jackie Davis; Joby Pauling; Tommy Clare, owner and coach driver; Chris McDonald; ?; Mr Harris (tailor); Archie Townsend; George Goatley.

SECTION TEN

Transport

1919. G.W.R. Station, Faringdon. From the time of the closure of the Faringdon spur to passenger traffic in the 1950s until the final closure of all traffic in 1963, Faringdon was used as a central distribution point for goods for the area — Wantage, Lambourne, Lechlade, Cirencester, Fairford, etc. The goods were brought to Faringdon Station by train and then distributed by lorry. The waiting room, on the left, still remains in use today as part of Scats farmers' wholesale store.

1912. G.W.R. Faringdon Station staff. Left to right, standing: Bill Bonner; — Case; W. MacKenzie; — Vaughan; ?; — Whiting; ?; J. Bowerman; ?; — Rawlings; ?. Sitting: ?; Mr Tidbury, Station Master; — Cook.

Old milestones on the Faringdon to Highworth road.

Elliott's steam tractor, 'Chaser', pulling a giant elm trunk.

The Market Place in 1953. The Town Hall in the centre was being used as a roundabout at this time. This was the beginning of the road protests in favour of a by-pass for Faringdon. There were parades and sit-downs in the road before a by-pass was agreed; it finally opened in 1974.

A firm had been laying a telephone cable and, in so doing, had damaged the old brick culvert taking the stream under the A420 through Faringdon. Sewage drains also went under the road and there was seepage of water and sewage. To inspect these pipes, use was made of TV cameras (one of the first times this happened) to discover what the damage was. It was found that bricks had collapsed from the brick culvert and were blocking the drains. At this time there was a lot of traffic passing through Faringdon; lorries from Pressed Steel were passing every two minutes, in addition to other traffic. The traffic could not be diverted or the road closed so it was decided to ask the army for help. The Ghurkas were given the job of erecting a Bailey Bridge over the road so that traffic could continue to use it while work carried on underneath. The road was closed from 6 p.m. on Saturday evening and re-opened at noon on the Sunday. The first vehicle to use it was the 2 p.m. bus from Oxford driven by Norman Skinner. The bus became stuck on the crown of the bridge as the incline was too steep, and had to be towed off. The incline was reduced and the traffic began to flow. However, the bridge was wide enough for two cars but not for two lorries, so traffic lights had to be put there because of the chaos caused with both traffic and pedestrians using the bridge. The work was completed in a week and then the bridge was removed. Jack Batten is the first adult from the right at the side of the ramp.

At one time the Town Hall was used to house both the Fire Brigade equipment and the ambulance.

1930. Faringdon Fire Brigade. Left to right, back standing: Dick Goddard; Sid Taylor; Herby Page; Archie Townsend; Mike Tucker. Front standing: Charlie Smith (Captain); – Drewett; H. Hunt; W. Busby; Chris Grey; Freddie Rogers. Sitting: Wilf Mulford (driver). The Fire Brigade had the use of a hand pump for many years; this was towed by horses and needed 14 men to operate it. About the 1920s, this pump was replaced by a mechanical pump which was towed by Anns' breakdown lorry, and then in 1930 the firemen had a collection and bought a motorised personnel carrier which they then used themselves.

c.1920. Faringdon Fire Brigade turning out to a fire at Kelmscott Manor Farm towed by Anns' breakdown vehicle. Mr Self (Captain) getting into the car. Harry Hancock climbing up to the front of the fire appliance.

SECTION ELEVEN

Views

Postage date 1911. The Folly Hill before the Tower was built and probably viewed from where Coxwell Gardens are now. The low roofed building third from the right is the ticket office of the railway station. Behind this is the goods shed and beyond is the workhouse in Union Street, now Ferndale Street.

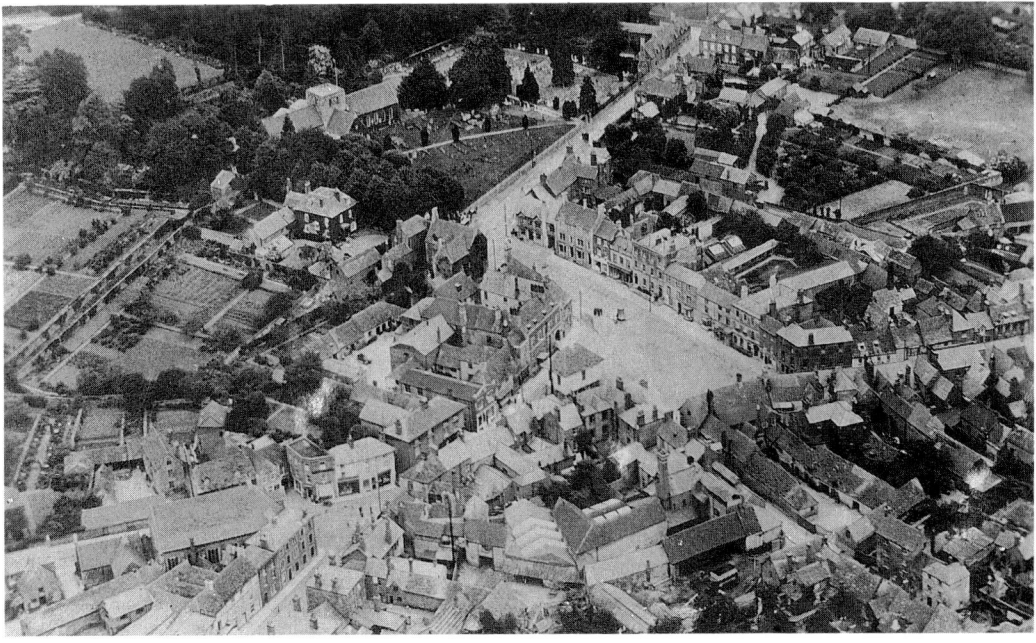

Aerial view over Faringdon town centre prior to 1936. The church, Faringdon House grounds and Audley House are easily recognised. Southampton Street, as we know it today, is virtually unrecognisable but the house opposite the car park is still there.

96 CHANGING FACES OF FARINGDON

1986. Grove Wood is at the top of the photograph and top right is Church Farm path. Just below are Sudbury Court houses under construction. At the centre bottom is Southampton Street with the Tourist Information caravan in the car park, its first venue in Faringdon.

1953. Faringdon viewed from the Folly Tower. The tall Dairy chimney in Park Road can easily be seen, along with the row of poplar trees which edged the Senior School in Southampton Street. The road just above the foreground trees is Stanford Road, with Tucker's Nursery and the old National School building on the corner.

SECTION TWELVE

Buscot

c.1920. Buscot Park House, from the north east showing the rose beds. This is the house in the time of the first Lord Faringdon before the alterations. The second Lord Faringdon altered the house drastically by demolishing the wings and many of the servants' quarters, which made the house much smaller.

1906. Wedding at Buscot Park Lodge. The Argent family at the wedding of Bessie Argent to George Grine. Left to right: Tom Argent, head forester for Lord Faringdon at Buscot Park; seated next is his wife who is holding Charlie Argent, the youngest of the family; seated in the front is Cyril Argent who, on the death of his father, became head forester for the estate.

1931 Buscot Park outing to Bournemouth, taken at Bournemouth. Left to right: Bert Dancy, the estate carpenter; Tommy Clare in the white coat, proprietor of Eagle Coaches; Gladys Davis; Mrs Ruth Argent, the wife of the head forester; Margaret Dancy, Bert's wife; Rev. Erward, Vicar of Buscot; a boy Edwards in front; Freddie Harris; behind him Mr Cyril Argent, the head forester; Mr Harry Sharps; in front of him Ernie Savory; Chum Hammond in a flat cap; Jeff Dancy, son of Bert and also a carpenter on the estate; Stan Sharps; Sid Rouse, carpenter; Rowland Dancy, son of Bert.

Early 1920s. Buscot Park stable yard. The photograph shows the entrance to the various coach houses with estate workers' flats above. The clock tower strikes the hours and only has a single hand. The entrance to the gardens is through the central doorway by the trap. The man standing by the bicycle is Thomas Argent, head forester.

THE BUSCOT PARK FLOWER SHOW

WILL BE HELD ON

THURSDAY, JULY 30TH, 1908

AT

BUSCOT PARK

(BY KIND PERMISSION OF SIR A. HENDERSON, BART.)

When the

GARDENS & GROUNDS

WILL BE THROWN OPEN TO THE PUBLIC.

THE

SWINDON TOWN MILITARY BAND

WILL BE IN ATTENDANCE.

DANCING after 6 o'clock in Roped Enclosure.

An Exhibition of the Celebrated **OXFORD ROSES**
(Kindly lent by Mr. GEORGE PRINCE, Longworth).

SWINGS, COCOANUT SHIES, BOWLING FOR PIGS.

SPORTS AT 3 P.M.

Tea and Refreshments will be supplied on the Ground by Mr. Hawkins, of Lechlade,
(At Moderate Prices).

ENTRANCE AT THE BUSCOT LODGE ONLY.   ADMISSION — 1 to 4 p.m., ONE SHILLING; 4 to 6, SIXPENCE; after 6, THREEPENCE.

Secretary — Mr. W. J. CAMBRIDGE, Eaton Hastings, Faringdon.

C. LUKER & CO. PRINTERS FARINGDON.

SECTION THIRTEEN

Coleshill

Looking up through the village. The whole village was owned by the Lord of the Manor, Lord Radnor, which meant that no alterations could go ahead without his permission and was known as a 'closed' village. Most of the cottages housed the estate workers.

Coleshill House built for Sir George Pratt and designed by one of Inigo Jones' pupils. The house had 365 windows, one for every day of the year. After WWII, the house became famous for the role it played in the training of people in subversive roles against a likely invasion by the Germans. It was a top secret establishment set up on the orders of Winston Churchill. Many people came here in secret, meeting at Highworth Post Office before being sent on a circuitous route to get to the house. Recently, an operational bunker was excavated and can be visited to see the conditions in which the secret army was supposed to work.

September 22nd 1952. Coleshill House on fire. The house had been handed over to the Ernest Cook Trust and was being completely re-decorated on the outside by a local firm of builders. A painter left a blow lamp burning on an attic window sill and went for his lunch; the lining of the window caught alight and set the house on fire. There was great difficulty in getting water to the fire because of its situation and the house was completely destroyed. Luckily, however, most of the interior furnishings were saved by the efforts of the local people and firemen. The only injuries sustained were to firemen who were burnt when molten lead dripped off the roof. The last fireman to leave the building was Faringdon's leading fireman, Sid Taylor. The picture shows a big turntable ladder at the top directing the hoses down into the centre of the building. The roof is completely gone and onlookers from the estate are just sadly looking at the remains of the house.

1890–1910 Coleshill Estate staff in the Estate yard.

SECTION FOURTEEN

Great Coxwell

An aerial photograph of the village taken from somewhere above the church. In the centre of the photograph, facing the camera, is a house called Crowdys. To the left of Crowdys is Green's farmhouse and then the Royal Oak public house (now closed). Behind the pub is Pear Tree Farm.

c.1910. The first building on the left-hand side was, until recently, the village Post Office. At one time it was a public house and the stone flagstones inside showed the wear of having barrels dragged through into the tap room.

GREAT COXWELL 103

c.1935. Pear Tree farmhouse. The strange looking car in the garden is Alldays and Onion's, but at this time it belonged to a man from London. The church tower of St. Mary's can be seen in the background.

> The Great Barn, Great Coxwell, near Faringdon.
>
> An interesting feature in the Village is an immense Barn, supposed to be the largest in the world, – on Court House Farm – which is 156 feet long and 45 feet wide. The Walls which are 4 feet thick, are supported by 28 buttresses; and the steep roof has rafters of 40 feet in length, which are supported by 10 huge uprights, resting on stone bases.

c.1905. The Great Barn belonging to the Cistercian monks who lived in the farmhouse. It was a Grange belonging to Beaulieu Abbey. The doorway on the side is the original one, the other is a modern alteration. The doorways at the ends of the building were inserted to accommodate the use of the wagons when the building was used as a farm barn.

The re-roofing of the Great Barn in the 1950s. The view is towards the farmhouse which was occupied by Mr A.B. Williams, a famous pig breeder. The barn is in the care of the National Trust and they decided that the roof needed repairing as there were many holes in it and much infestation of woodworm in the timbers. An architect from Stanford was engaged, the work being undertaken by Pether & Sons from Burford. They erected scaffolding and completely stripped the stone slates from the roof. New timbers were inserted where it was absolutely necessary, the whole wooden structure was treated for woodworm and other wood boring insects and then the tiles replaced. It was a long, tedious job and work was continued throughout the winter in order to complete it on time.

SECTION FIFTEEN

Little Coxwell

Early 1920s. Looking up from the old A420 link road towards the Eagle pub, which is just out of shot. The cottages were pulled down when Mr Jeffrey Berners bought the Grove estate to build modern houses for the workers.

1942. A wartime meet of the Hunt. Jack Pickford, huntsman, leading the hounds down into the village. The main road is in the distance.

1940s. Mr and Mrs P.J. Smith, a headmaster who was evacuated with his school from London to this area during WWII.

A Little Coxwell School group in 1947. The class teacher is Miss Vera Knapp.

SECTION SIXTEEN

Eaton Hastings

1915. The village of Eaton Hastings was originally by the river but became a deserted medieval village. These houses, known as New Buildings, were built by the first Lord Faringdon when he bought the estate in the 1880s. The photograph shows the village shop and Post Office with Miss Apse the postmistress outside, and the village children on both sides of the road. The land was low lying and liable to flood and this is why the pavement was high to act as a causeway; it was known by that name for many years.

The Anchor Inn about 1970. This was a remote pub by the River Thames crossing. Unfortunately, in a tragic accident, it was burnt down and the landlord and his partner died. The fire was caused by the dog's tail waving in front of the gas heater.

SECTION SEVENTEEN

Fernham

High Street in 1915. The first cottage is the village shop and Post Office run by David Brown. In front of the shop was Mrs Brighton, wife of the chauffeur at Ringdale Manor, with her children Ray, Bern and Sean. The building directly behind them was a coal and candle store. The owner would collect coal harnessed to a little handcart from Uffington Station. He would deliver ½ cwt of coal to anywhere in Faringdon at any time, day or night, for 2/6d. The next building is the barn belonging to the Woodman Inn, used by the local undertaker and wheelwright. Behind the barn is the Woodman Inn with stables, and some farm buildings belonging to a farmhouse which stood on the corner. The house in the distance was known as the Red House which was at one time a public house known as the Black Horse. It was the only house in Fernham with a cellar.

Early 1930s. The old Post Office, which was probably the old manor house with a beautiful staircase inside. In the background is Peach Tree Cottage.

The village green in 1910 showing the village pump with the cover over the top. The cottage behind the pump is still there and behind that was the old village school which closed just before the First World War. The church was built by public subscription and opened in 1861 after the vicar of Longcot purchased some land in Fernham, with his own money, because he felt sorry for his parishioners having to walk all the way to Longcot church.

1920. The Village Pump on the green. It is an old lead pump with a wooden casing over a very old bottle well (a stone well shaped like a wine bottle). The well itself is about 12–15ft deep. The wife of the vicar of Longcot (the same one who had the church built) felt sorry for the women fetching water and so had a cover put over it.

1930. The house called Thatchetts at the end of Church Lane with Nancy Warner standing in the doorway. She was the daughter of a seamstress who had a couple of apprentices and quite a thriving business.

Mrs Gilling, with Ray and Kitty (later Mrs Edward Green of Sands Farm), standing in front of Fernham Farm House in 1914. The original farmhouse, pulled down in the 1960s, was on the farm itself. These two cottages were converted into one for the farm manager when the farm was owned by a Swindon man.

Peach Cottage c.1925 with Mrs Seaford cleaning the doorstep. She lived there for many years and was mother of Lil Fuller.

1960s. In the tap room of the Woodman Inn. On the left is Bill Dabney, a Fernham man, who worked at Manor Farm for George Adams. With him is Hector McFarling, from the Channel Islands, who worked as a groom for Mr Fieldgate, the local vet. He also worked for Mr Adams and ended his working life at Abingdon aerodrome.

c.1910 at Fernham Farm. On the hayrick is Sam Lawrence and those standing are, from left to right: the farm manager from Swindon; Billy Muggins; — Mildenhall. The Maundrell elevator was built in Calne. The shaft leading from the elevator goes to a horse gin, which is a primitive type of engine where gearing was fixed to the ground by the strike and a horse walked round and round and provided the motor power for the elevator to take the hay up onto the rick.

Jack Warner of Peach Tree Cottage, an ex-market gardener, with his adopted granddaughter in the 1950s.

SECTION EIGHTEEN

Shellingford

In the early 1900s, the Henderson family of Kitemore House replaced some old cottages in Church Street with these new houses. There were twelve houses altogether built in blocks of 3,4,3 and 2. The stone was quarried from Bowling Alley Copse, The Slade, Stanford.

Looking up Church Street in 1910. The houses shown in the previous photograph are now completed.

Looking down Church Street. Notice the lady drawing water at the standpipe on the left. The old cottage next to the Post Office no longer exists. Church Farm house, on the right, is owned by Mr David Gantlett who took it over from his father, Mr Reginald Gantlett. Previously the farm belonged to Mr Maidment.

SHELLINGFORD 115

St. Faith's Church. It was re-roofed in 1939 because of damage caused by the Death Watch Beetle.

Spectators to a Society Wedding from Kitemore House in 1907. The Green family are in the pony trap on the left.

A 1952 view of the Reading Room, formerly a cottage used as a mens' meeting room, later used as a dinner room for the schoolchildren. It was pulled down and the area used to make a drive-in access to Church Cottage. In the background is the spire of the Church, the top of which was replaced with one made of fibre glass, when it became unsafe.

This cottage was occupied by Mr and Mrs George Mitchell until 1932 when they moved to 4 Church Street. George was a shoemaker and repairer and carried on his trade in part of the cottage. This building was eventually condemned and pulled down.

The marriage on August 6th 1907 of Gertrude Pill and Alfred Potter at 7 Church Street (the end house shown in the previous picture). Left to right, back row: Ernest Pill; George Pill; Henry Pill; – Stock; Thomas Pill; W. Potter, best man; Fred Pill; Jack Pill. Middle row: Peggy Pill (George's wife); Florrie Pill; Annie Stock, née Pill; Elizabeth (Lizzie) Pill; Louie Pill, née Shepherd (Fred's wife); Rosetta Pill (Jack's wife); husband of bridegroom's sister. Front Row: Bessie Pill (Ernest's wife); Ellen Pill, née Stallard (great grandmother); Alfred Potter (bridegroom); Gertrude Pill (bride); George Pill (great grandfather); Beatrice Pill; bridegroom's sister (Miss Potter?); William Pill jnr and Ernest Pill jnr (children of Ernest and Bessie).

1920s. Fred Pill, son of Henry, shearing sheep.

c.1920. John (Jack) Pill, shepherd, brother of Henry.

Alfred George Pill, roadman, with his tricycle in the early 1930s. He was born at Thrupp and brought up in Shellingford. He lived for some time at Fernham and then moved back to Shellingford. For many years he was a Congregational Lay Preacher.

Mr Bartholomew and Milly Mitchell. Mr Bartholomew lodged with Mr and Mrs Mitchell from 1931 to 1932. He was employed felling timber in the Wilderness; this is now arable land.

The 1937 Coronation festivities. Left-hand picture: Milly and Bill Mitchell. Right-hand picture: Doris and Kathleen Rixon.

120 CHANGING FACES OF FARINGDON

George Mitchell and his beehives in the garden of 4 Church Street.

Pat Fourte and Milly Mitchell with Tom Draper, cowman to Cecil Gantlett and Victor Draper, in 1939 or 1940.

Mrs Jacobs and her daughter Gladys on October 14th 1956. Mr Jacobs and his father, originally from Norfolk, were gamekeepers for the Kitemore Estate. They lived first at the Timberyard Cottages, later moving to 6 Church Street.

SECTION NINETEEN

Uffington

Uffington Wharf c.1907. The bridge over the Wilts and Berks Canal on the Fernham/Uffington road. A postman with a bicycle is standing on the bridge. The photographer is on the Fernham bank. In the event of a barge wishing to pass along the canal, the bridge was lifted by beams which were counter-weighted so that it would stay in the upright position. If anyone, coming along from the Fernham direction, wished to cross the bridge and it was still upright, there was a long pole with a hook on the end which was hooked onto a ring at the end of the bridge and the person heaved the bridge down. The building in the background was called Wharf Farm and was occupied by Mr Jenkins. He was a haulier with a team of white horses and worked for the Astor Estate. Mr Jenkins also ran a small farm. He was the last man to have a barge at Uffington, using it for hauling coal from Swindon to Wantage on the small section of the canal that was still in use. The barge was last used to transport hay to the farm. It was then left to rot in the water and its remains are still in the base of the canal which has now been filled in and a modern bungalow built on top.

122 CHANGING FACES OF FARINGDON

The Packer family, wheelwright and blacksmith, and staff in the High Street in front of the forge. The baby being carried was Queenie Weaver who became the cook at Uffington school.

1890s. Uffington Castle on an August Monday. The people were brought up the hill by the horse-drawn vehicles in the background. Note the children playing with a cart in the foreground. Uffington Hill was the usual destination for outings at this time.

Westminster Bridge Cottage on Woolstone Road. The owners also had a small paddock across the road in which they raised pigs and hens.

On the left are Mr James Pike and his wife Susannah standing outside their butcher's shop. They had arrived from somewhere in the Midlands early in the 20th century. On the right are their daughter and son-in-law, Mr and Mrs Norton.

Mr and Mrs Pike's daughter, Mrs Norton, standing in the doorway of her general store and post office in 1939. She was the second generation of the family to own the shop (see the previous picture). The billboards outside are all concerned with the events leading up to the Second World War.

Uffington Station c.1897. The single track branch line to Faringdon is on the left. The photographer is standing on the bridge looking down onto the workshop buildings. Water was piped, under the Faringdon track, from a spring on Ringdale Hill to the tower on the left. The Junction Hotel is on the right in the background. The staff are lined up on the crossing between the 'up' and 'down' platforms.

1937 Coronation Celebrations. The Craven Estate fire engine, which was kept in Uffington. A popular story in the village was that if you were single and had a ride on the fire engine you would be married within the year. The engine is preserved and kept at Newbury Museum. Left to right: Joyce Bowley; Mrs Queenie Weaver; Ettie Lewer; ?; ?; ?; ?; Mrs Dainty snr; Mrs George Weaver; ?; ?; Mrs Susan Packer.

The Craven Estate timberyard. The fire engine house is the building next to the left-hand cottage. In the timberyard is a selection of tree trunks or 'sticks' as they were known. These would have been of oak, ash or elm. All the sawing was done by hand over a saw-pit. The sawyer stood on top of the log and guided the saw to the trunk line, while the labourer stood in the pit and pulled the saw down, getting covered in sawdust. The head of the yard is the man standing in the centre with his foot on a log.

Broad Street pre-1907. The man is Mr Kosser who ran the Post Office and Village Store and was also the local postman. He was of German extraction and at the outbreak of the First World War, when there was a great deal of anti-German feeling, he changed the spelling of his name to Cosser.

The rear of the Baker's Arms taken from the lane leading to the church. It is thought to be the birthplace of John Hughes, forebear of Thomas Hughes of *Tom Brown's Schooldays* fame.

The High Street, before 1906, looking down into the centre of the village. A crowd of people in front of Packers, the builders, on the left-hand side. The lady in the black dress with the white apron standing in the centre of the road is 'Granny' Maria Packford.

A Conservative Fete held in the early 1900s on the field where the new village hall now stands. The Kingston Lisle Brass Band is on the raised dais in the centre.

Broad Street in the 1920s or 1930s showing the new School with the schoolmaster's house attached. The original school was the Tom Brown School and is now the Uffington Museum.

An Uffington School group in 1952 with the teacher, Miss Jarrett, at the rear. Left to right, back row: George Switzer; Sheila Reynolds; Andy McBain; Jennifer Ritchings; Fred Smith; Barbara Gorton; Betty Chainey; ?; Clive Avenell; Carol Mattingley; James Collett. Middle row: Christine –; Brenda Avenell; Christine Whitehorn; Jane Attrill; Jackie Miller; ?; Kathy Wickell; Brenda Dainty; Valerie Avenell; ?; ?; Jemmy Trump. Front row: Freddie Challis; James Aldridge; ?; John Reynolds; Brian Chainey; David Connors; Anthony Keen; 'Tiggy' Packford; Alan Peacock.

The Mildenhall family who lived on the Fawler road and were small farmers. Albert James Mildenhall and his wife Elizabeth had five sons (Herbert, Arthur, Albert who died in infancy, Albert, Wilfred) and four daughters (Margaret, Rosa, Dora, Florence). The eldest son rose through the ranks in the army to become an officer and was one of the first men to drive the new tanks in the First World War.

Shotover Corner c.1915. The photographer was standing in the High Street, looking towards the road leading to the White Horse Hill. The cottages in the background are now known as Shotover House. There have been very few changes in the view since this was taken.